The Uncertain Crusade

The Uncertain Crusade
America and the Russian Revolution of 1905

ARTHUR W. THOMPSON & ROBERT A. HART

THE UNIVERSITY OF MASSACHUSETTS PRESS

Preface

AMONG THE MANY reform movements of America's Progressive Era, none was more energetically undertaken than democratization of Russia. In early 1905 newspaper editors in every section of the country were calling for crusades against Nicholas II. Church congregations heard bellicose sermons, then sang "Onward, Christian Soldiers." Young men volunteered to cross the ocean and fight the Cossacks. Citizens' committees raised money to support revolution in Russia and collected signatures on petitions which demanded of President Theodore Roosevelt a wide assortment of diplomatic and military actions against the Tsar.

The fanfare of commitment was so shrill that it could be heard in Russia's peasant villages, workers' slums, and Jewish ghettos, where people came to believe that help was on the way.

Unfortunately for the hopes of revolutionaries, theirs was a passing vogue. Within a single year American enthusiasm gave way to doubt, disillusionment, and finally to outright hostility. This study presents several aspects of that shift from one extreme to another, a reversal manifestly apparent by the end of 1905, when it became the subject of many a heated comment both in Russia and in the United States.

Fund-raising drives faltered, as did other programs which had been undertaken in the name of Russian reforms. Public derision replaced the adulation that had greeted revolutionary emissaries earlier in the year. While the present authors have not attempted a detailed study of public opinion—seeking instead to examine several aspects of America's response to Russian events—they have noted a definite shift in the editorial opinion of general-circulation newspapers and magazines. Of fifty-six such publications consulted, forty-nine favored the revolution in January 1905; and by the end of the year, forty-two of the forty-nine had altered their position to one of opposition.

After their cause failed, disappointed Russian revolutionaries selected the United States as a target for scornful comment. Criticism from Russia was viewed as ironic and grossly unfair, for Americans believed that they had surpassed the people of all other nations in praising the revolution and in promising to support it, and they should be given credit for having meant well, even though their enthusiasm had produced no practical results.

Why was the United States so despised in Russia? Newspapermen asked this question of Paul Miliukov, historian and disappointed revolutionary, when he visited New York in 1908. He spoke at length about the distribution of false hopes, hands of friendship offered then withdrawn, and language undisciplined by concern over its consequences. Russians who had believed the early promises quite naturally resented their nonfulfillment.

Some of Miliukov's interviewers inferred that he was criticizing America's ability to act, or even the courage of her people. Not so, the historian insisted. He said that he could respect any nation that chose to act, or not to act, in accordance with its own interests. He admitted that interests, from the viewpoint of the United States government, had not included involvement on the side of Russia's revolution. The problem lay in the making, not the breaking, of the promise. The former had been avoidable, the latter not.

Democratic idealism, Puritan intensity, romanticism, sentimentalism, moralism, evangelism, sense of mission, crusaders' zeal—labels abound as modern historians try to explain why verbal overcommitment has become an American diplomatic tradition. To the numerous affairs that have illustrated this unfortunate tradition may be added the response of the United States to the Russian revolution of 1905.

I was not acquainted with Professor Arthur W. Thompson, of the University of Florida, who died shortly after having finished research on America's response to the 1905 revolution. It was my good fortune to have been invited to write a book based upon this extensive research, and I can only hope that the result would have pleased Professor Thompson. I am most grateful to Mrs. Irene Thompson for giving me the opportunity to complete her husband's work, and to Professor Howard H. Quint, of the University of Massachusetts Department of History, for valuable advice touching several areas of the study. I also wish to thank the National Foundation on the Arts and Humanities, Washington, D.C., for a grant in behalf of this work.

The authors are also indebted to Mrs. Mary G. Siegel, for translations from Russian and Yiddish newspapers, and to others who aided Professor Thompson in his research: Mr. Norman Thomas and Mrs. Vladimir Woytinsky for interviews; Mr. Upton Sinclair and Mr. Morris D. Waldman for correspondence; staffs of the National Archives, the Manuscript Division of the Library of Congress, numerous public and private repositories of papers; and publishers who permitted quotations from Vladimir S. Woytinsky's *Stormy Passage* (Vanguard Press, Inc.), and Richard Hough's *The Potemkin Mutiny* (Hamish Hamilton, Ltd.).

ROBERT A. HART
University of Massachusetts
November 1969

Contents

The Uncertain Crusade

Plehve

1. The Challenge of Russia

AT THE BEGINNING of the twentieth century Americans
entered what many called an Age of Progress, and they
were confident, even cheerful, about the prospect of heavy
burdens to be imposed upon them. There were challenges to
be met, problems to be solved, and wrongs to be righted.
Platitudes of moral outrage were replacing those of self-
satisfaction, a change of mood that was creating the Progressive Era, remarkable for the quantity, if not the quality,
of reforms in politics, government, industry, and urban life.

Reformers also had time for unsolved problems abroad.
Among foreign imperfections—European encroachments in
China, Britain's treatment of Ireland, sufferings of natives
in the Congo, and continued wrongdoing (as Theodore
Roosevelt put it) in Latin American nations—none could
compare with those of Russia. Drawing on such words as
intolerable, unbelievable, unthinkable, and unspeakable,
newspapermen confessed their inability to adequately describe the Tsarist regime. They tried as best they could,

presenting lurid details against a backdrop of Gothic reds and blacks. Americans read how policemen set fire to huts of suspected revolutionaries and waited in darkness to shoot down those trying to escape the flames. Casualties always ran high among children and grandmothers, according to the newspapers. "Their eyes burned feverishly in the dungeon shadows," the Associated Press said of prisoners confined in the Fortress of Peter and Paul.[1] Seeking colorful contrasts, editors sometimes penciled in snow, in one case applying this technique to a summer massacre in the Crimea. If one hundred Jews had been slain in a pogrom, digits could be added at random, improving a headline's impact and excused by the general assumption that no one could really know what went on in vast and mysterious Russia.

Nicholas II (in reality a timid creature vacillating under pressures from wife, ministers, clergy, nobility, and his own mixed feelings about duties to his people and to the antique system he had sworn to preserve) was portrayed as an arch-fiend in most American publications. Ugly, brutal, and sinister, he was said to have brandished whips and sabers instead of the croquet mallets so often mentioned by later biographers. His very existence was an affront—to democracy because he was an autocrat, to progress because he was an anachronism, and to morality because he was the embodiment of all things evil. According to the *Cincinnati Enquirer*, the Tsar represented a challenge to everything Americans held most dear.[2]

Because Nicholas was intolerable, a George III in American eyes, revolution was considered to be the only way to deal with him: Could not his subjects understand this? How could they endure the miseries he imposed upon them for another day, another month, another year? Editorialists had been predicting revolution for two decades, and by 1904 their loathing for the Tsar was nearly matched by their impatience with the Russian people. Journalists asserted that the "people" must act at once to overthrow tyranny; the "people" must create their own 1776 without further delay. Advising against oversimplification, thoughtful commentators pointed to deep divisions among peasants, factory workers, Western-style liberals, and members of national and religious minorities. Russians had only their discontent in common. Revolution might be predictable, but its political outcome could hardly be known.

Most Russians were peasants, causing some foreign observers to say that millions of Pugachevs would sweep out of the hinterlands and engulf the seats of government. Land reforms had been ignored, sales taxes were high, and famine was a chronic condition. In 1904, about one family in three worked its own farm, a decreased percentage from previous years because farmers were unable to meet payments and to compete with owners of large estates, who could afford to purchase iron plows and hire experts on scientific farming. Those peasants interested in politics sometimes gathered to hear speeches by members of the Social Revolutionary (SR) party. Mostly university students, these spokesmen of change risked freezing blizzards, attacks by wolves, and the Cossack's sword as they made their way from village to village. Their greatest enemy, they frequently complained, was rural dull-wittedness, but it was not always a peasant's fault if he failed to comprehend the SR message. Most party members believed in a vague, romantic socialism. Making clear their opposition to the evolutionary doctrines of Karl Marx, they claimed that the ideal state was immediately attainable. SRs opposed each other mainly on the question of tactics. On one extreme, a speaker might advocate nonviolence, Christian humility, and the signing of humbly phrased petitions to the Tsar. A month later another SR speaker might advise the same audience to assassinate all government officials in accordance with the program of the party's militant wing, the Organization of Combat.

Compared to the peasantry, the urban proletariat was much smaller in numbers but better organized and more precise in its doctrines. Industrialization had begun in earnest by the 1870s. Landless peasants came to cities in search of jobs, accepting meager wages and twelve-hour working days, and trying to adjust to life in the bleak slums that surrounded each cluster of factory chimneys. Depressions drove many workers back to the country, where at least they could starve in pastoral surroundings. Others risked hanging by joining illegal trade unions, and some came to admire the Marxism of the Social Democratic (SD) party. While SDS ridiculed the incoherent goals and tactics of peasant revolutionaries, most were willing to work temporarily with any group powerful enough to be of help in toppling the Tsar. SDS felt that the present system, which they called feudalistic, should be replaced by liberal capitalism in the Western style, the excesses of which would automatically create a proletarian revolution.

SRS and SDS were considered a shabby lot by Americans, few of whom could make sense of their strange and contradictory doctrines. It was convenient to ignore them and look forward to a more familiar type of revolution.

This too was possible. Along with a proletariat, Russian industrialization had created a small but influential business class. Its representatives, supported by doctors, lawyers, and most university teachers, spoke hopefully of civil rights, parliaments, and even democracy. The more conservative liberals begged the Tsar to reveal his fundamental decency by granting reforms in such a way that he would retain his throne in the English fashion. Americans preferred another type of liberal who considered monarchy useless and looked to the United States rather than to Great Britain as a model to be copied. These anti-Tsar liberals condoned terrorism by peasants as well as strikes and riots by labor, all of which would supply the raw power necessary for the success of revolution, the results of which would be controlled and shaped by liberals.

American sympathies were also drawn to minority groups,

both national and religious, whose individuality was often brutally suppressed by the Russian government. In its attempts to Russify such provinces as Poland, Courland, and Finland, the government operated a ruthless system of coercion. Removal of the tongue, for example, was a favored punishment for persons refusing to speak the Russian language. Similar attempts to impose religious orthodoxy only increased revolutionary sentiment among Jews, Protestants, and Roman Catholics. In the considered opinion of Konstantin Pobedonostsev, Procurator of the Holy Synod and advisor to the Tsar, the government's risk was slightest when its victims were Jews. Pogroms were often used to suppress general dissatisfactions among the masses. The government's role in pogroms did not have to be direct. It gave official blessing to the Black Hundreds, patriotic societies dedicated to reducing the Jewish population by a third in hopes the rest might be inspired to accept Christianity or emigrate to America. In 1903 Minister of Interior Viacheslav von Plehve ordered free distribution of Zionist plot pamphlets and vodka to the citizens of Kishinev. Police and soldiers made no effort to stop the massacre that followed.[3]

Government officials saw war, as well as pogroms, as a means of easing the pressure of internal discontent. Conflict began in early 1904 with a Japanese attack on the naval base at Port Arthur. Russia had done much to provoke the attack, partly through greed for more territory in Manchuria and Korea and partly as a device for developing loyalty to the Tsar. "The country is on the brink of revolution," Plehve said, "and the one thing that can stop it is a small, victorious war."[4] The calculated gamble was based largely on longstanding European contempt for Oriental military abilities. In case of surprise—war that was neither small nor victorious—results at home could be catastrophic.

Revolutionaries of all factions had been looking abroad for help, and many now placed their hopes in the Japanese army and navy. Others were sceptical of the small nation's chances and hoped to enlist the aid of Europe's democracies. Certain reform groups in England were showing interest (although never so excitedly as in the United States), and encouraging pronouncements came from radical parties in France. Yet it was clear that the governments of these nations, concerned about the possibility of war with the Central Powers, did not welcome upheaval in Russia. The British government issued reminders that its 1902 alliance with Japan, which protected the signatories against attack by two or more powers, would not be effective so long as Japan fought only the Tsar. In 1904 Britain formed an entente with France, a nation already tied to Nicholas by treaty and by heavy financial investments in his regime. Nor could the Central Powers tolerate revolution (even one promising disruption of a rival alliance) against a political system so like their own. The emperors of Germany and Austria-Hungary even offered to lend the Tsar police and army units to help quell the threat of revolution.

Although European diplomacy supported the *status quo* in Russia, revolutionaries inferred something entirely different where the United States was concerned. They came to believe that America would aid their cause with money, munitions, volunteers, diplomatic support, and perhaps even military intervention.

This faith in the United States was based on the belief that Americans were perennial champions of freedom. For more than a century they had advertised what they variously called their tradition, heritage, manifest destiny, special responsibility, and unique purpose in the world.

In 1793, when France was trying to preserve her revolution against the combined monarchies of Europe, citizen Edmond Genêt arrived from France in Charleston, South Carolina, with two favors to ask: Would Americans volunteer for armies he planned to lead against British Canada and Spanish Louisiana? Would they provide privateers for raids against British shipping? To both questions the answer was yes, exuberantly so, expressed by crowds that cheered Genêt, by local politicians who pounded his back and filled him with Carolina whisky, and by Thomas Jefferson, who believed that the outcome of the French Revolution would determine the success or failures of democracy everywhere on earth.[5] But public enthusiasm could not always be trusted. If Genêt remained untaught by recent occurrences in his own country, he learned the lesson well when he reached Philadelphia. President George Washington coldly rebuffed all appeals by the Frenchman, even those dramatized with flowing tears and temper tantrums. Genêt was shocked by the president's failure to be moved by the desperate plight of America's sister republic: Had he forgotten his own great debt to France, a nation that had sent men and money to help him win another revolution a few years earlier? Washington made it clear to Genêt that he saw no necessary connection between sentiment and diplomatic practice. The obligation to France, the president put it bluntly, simply was not worth the risk of involvement in Europe's great war. Hearing of Genêt's treatment, America's pro-French faction howled that the United States government was ignoring public opinion and a moral duty. Concerned about what the French people would think, Americans feared that they would be called hardhearted, ungrateful, and even cowardly. Genêt would be thoroughly disillusioned, and for this the Francophiles blamed Washington rather than themselves, for he had broken their promises.

In 1821 Greece rebelled against Turkish rule. Here was a fascinating heroine, "the mother of democracy calling for help from her children everywhere." The villain was doubly despised by Americans as a despot and a heathen, who, as everyone knew, collected Greek ears in large baskets. Clergymen told Americans not to forget their sacred duty. Orators, among them Daniel Webster, spoke of democratic duties to be performed in memory of Socrates, Pericles, and Demosthenes. Edward Everett's "Greek Appeal" raised several thousand dollars, but Everett spent much of this on Bibles and was later criticized for not having shipped munitions instead. "I dreamed that Greece might still be free," Lord Byron wrote, inspiring dozens of young Americans to go there and die beside him. Congress debated a possible role for the government—financial, diplomatic, or military—but never acted. Secretary of State John Quincy Adams often reminded enthusiasts that the United States was not yet physically capable of fighting a war in the eastern Mediterranean. Idealism was also dampened by reports of Greek atrocities against Turks. The *Boston Recorder* stated with evident relief, "We were ready to help Greece, but now she no longer deserves that help."[6]

An old friend of the United States, the Marquis de Lafayette, led French citizens against the Bourbon monarchy in July 1830. The remarkably successful coup required no more than two days of fighting. Romantic novelist James Fenimore Cooper, traveling in Germany at the time, kissed his wife good-by and boarded a fast coach for Paris. He arrived too late to be of service, as did Washington Irving, who had hurried over from London. The revolution was "warmly greeted in every part of the United States," *Niles' Weekly Register* observed, "with not a hint of dissent." Bourbon effigies went up in flames, and President Andrew Jackson marched at the head of a parade in honor of French freedom. Disappointment came with news that Lafayette had placed another king, Louis-Philippe, on the vacant throne. The *National Intelligencer* complained, "France has passed up a golden opportunity to erect an American-style republic, hailed everywhere on earth as the most successful form of government in God's firmament of nations."[7]

In 1845 John O'Sullivan, editor of the *United States Magazine*, coined the term "manifest destiny" to justify a national urge to extend democracy by force of arms to Mexican and British holdings in North America. Other patriots used the phrase in a global sense, calling for active American participation in revolutions that swept over Europe beginning in 1848. "We shall rejoice to see our American model upon the Lower Danube," asserted Secretary of State Daniel Webster, full of whisky at a Hungarian freedom rally.[8] Even so, Webster sometimes worried about unfamiliar philosophies which seemed to have intruded into certain causes abroad.

When Germans, Frenchmen, Italians, and Hungarians crossed the Atlantic to ask for money, they were careful to oversimplify revolutionary ideologies. Their goal was always freedom, and the opposition always monarchy. They desired precisely those ends, they said, that Americans had so courageously won from George III. James Buchanan told an applauding audience that these were "glorious revolutions." Henry Wadsworth Longfellow wrote, "So long as a king is left upon his throne there will be no justice on earth." Thousands of copies of the Constitution were dispatched to European trouble spots. Revolutionaries, who wanted more than words, drew encouragement from mass meetings in Boston, New York, Philadelphia, and Cincinnati, where orators demanded war upon all despots. Many believed that America's invincible armies, having recently liberated the northern half of Mexico, would embark for central Europe and grant Hungarians the gift of freedom.[9]

Louis Kossuth, a Hungarian revolutionist on tour in the United States, heard the same promises of support at every banquet. Equally tiresome to him were the grand balls and torchlight parades, the Hungarian seedcakes hosts invariably fed him, the gypsy dances they had played for him, and their manner of copying a celebrity's cut of mustache and style of dress. At last he felt compelled to say that, while he was enjoying himself immensely, the purpose of his mission was to obtain "financial, material, and political aid." Following the collection of several thousand dollars, an astonished Kossuth saw his sponsors spend most of it on more banquets and parades.[10]

Often the government appeared to be on the verge of some deed that could benefit the 1848 revolutions. Excitement generated by the press and by prorevolutionary speakers made it impossible for diplomats to remain calm at all times. The State Department prematurely recognized a republican government in France; ministers discharged random insults in European courts; and Secretary Webster's personal declaration of war on Austria came to nothing due to Vienna's tolerant assumption that he had written it while under the influence of intoxicants. In the end, Kossuth's mission was a failure, as was his revolution. Calling himself sick with disappointment, he made statements implying that Americans were not to be trusted, and these in turn elicited anger, mystification, and ruminations over Hungarian ingratitude.[11]

The Civil War complicated the revolutionary heritage. Europeans, somewhat weary of publicity on the subject, took delight in pointing out that the Confederacy was engaged in a cause which bore remarkable resemblance to that of 1776. Was not the South fighting for the right to determine its own political destiny, and the North attempting to crush this bid for freedom? British journalists compared Abraham Lincoln with George III, and Jefferson Davis with Thomas Jefferson. For strategic reasons—the desire not to drive border states out of the Union—Northerners could not answer such charges by openly proclaiming emancipation of slaves to be a war aim. It was not until January 1863, when President Lincoln announced the Emancipation Proclamation, that Americans were able to say that their heritage remained unchanged. The United States was still the champion of freedom, even while repressing a revolution. Southerners, with their clearly objectionable cause, were teaching the nation that not all revolutions were the same. Some were good and others bad; some must be encouraged and others crushed.

A workingmen's rebellion in France offered further proof that unwholesome qualities could be present in some revolutions. The Commune controlled Paris for ten weeks in early

1871. Its radical goals prompted American newspapermen to rediscover a vocabulary that had not been applied to revolutionary activity since the eighteenth century, when Federalist publications had attacked French Jacobinism. "The mob," a favorite term among European monarchists in 1848, now found wide use in the United States. The men of the Commune—called malcontents, devils, vile elements, and monsters from the sewers—threatened to ruin Paris, according to American newsmen. Here was a "socialistic outbreak," the *New York Times* said, "a stroke at property itself." The *Chicago Tribune* detected "a shudder through all Christendom," not excluding Chicago in view of the *Tribune*'s shocking descriptions of revolutionary rapes and murders. Many editors used Commune excesses to justify attacks upon the labor union movement in the United States.[12]

Once more before the end of the century the nation found a revolution that deserved support. No dime novelist could have created a plot more romantic, more sentimental, more satisfying in its simplicity, than that provided by Cuba's struggle with Spain in 1898. Not since Turkey's assault on Greece had there appeared an enemy more perfect than Spain—monarchical, aristocratic, undemocratic, snobbish, unprogressive, cowardly, and corrupt, according to a compilation in the *New York Journal*. A symbol of all Spanish imperfections was "Butcher" Weyler, the commander in Cuba. Correspondents described him as operating concentration camps, firing squads, and strange torture devices no doubt left over from the Inquisition. Seeking increased circulation, the tabloids specialized in maiden-in-distress stories, making it quite clear that a rescuer was needed.[13] While several motives were present in the clamor for war, the most highly publicized was that popular urge to fight for freedom in behalf of an oppressed people. This time there were no prohibitive reasons—geographic, diplomatic, or military—why pressure from the press could not be allowed to influence official policy.

Russian revolutionary leaders drew hopeful inferences from the Spanish-American War of 1898, as well as from recently successful fund-raising campaigns in behalf of the Russian Jews and the Congolese, efforts indicating that American responses to problems abroad were not always romantic and meaningless. Yet Paul Miliukov, who was an historian as well as a revolutionary, must have been aware that talk had been far more important than action in the development of that American heritage upon which he was now placing his hopes.

This uncertain heritage was not the only source for high expectations in Russia. It was apparent to the whole world that Americans had entered an exceptionally robust period of their national life. Reform rhetoric knew no restraints. Furious over the existence of a wide assortment of intolerable conditions, progressives were placing no limit on the number of changes they demanded.

They had accomplished much by 1904. President Theodore Roosevelt, building a reputation as a trust buster, had broken a number of industrial monopolies. His Elkins Act struck at railroad empires, and he was mounting an attack upon corporation practices that ruined streams and forests. He made a start on legislation aimed at regulating drug and meat-packing industries. The presidential mood helped inspire other reform programs. Laboring men, clubwomen, clergymen, professors, and even some businessmen formed tentative alliances that put pressure on all levels of government. Cleveland and Toledo (Ohio) were first among municipalities to pass laws weakening the power of political machines. Wisconsin led a movement among states to institute referendum, initiative, direct primaries, secret ballots, and other devices aimed at making government more responsive to the people. Maryland adopted workmen's compensation in 1902, and Oregon decreed in 1903 that women should work no more than ten hours a day in factories.

In case of weariness or boredom, a reformer could revive

the driving force of his indignation by reading practically any issue of *McClure's, Collier's, Cosmopolitan,* or the *American.* Among the revolution's attractive qualities was its appeal to progressive writers. Looking over a vast array of dark events in Russia, journalists could find effective analogies for domestic targets. Persons who considered Roosevelt's reforms too mild said that he was a timid Tsar, manipulated by the grand dukes of the Republican party. (Those who objected to trust busting applied to the president all lately popular synonyms for autocratic despotism.) America's recent suppression of revolution in the Philippine Islands was compared with the methods of Russian imperialism. Political bosses grew in notoriety through comparison with the Tsar. The *Commoner* said, "Quite a number of free Americans, who cannot understand why the Russian people submit to the rule of Grand Dukes and other nobles, go right ahead accepting the political bossism of men like Platt, Aldrich, Depew, Cannon, Beveridge, and others." Americans enjoyed about as much voice in their government as Ukrainians, said one editor in advocating popular election of United States senators. And it was a popular view that not until all states adopted the secret ballot would Americans have more liberty than Muscovites. "Russia may be ripe for self-government, but we are over-ripe," said a Florida paper. Prohibition societies also discovered analogies: "The Tsar is always drunk, and look at the kind of man he is." Equally reprehensible to prohibitionists was the distribution of vodka for pogroms, not much different from the way American politicians served their own interests with free beer on election days.[14]

Men such as J. P. Morgan, John D. Rockefeller, the Vanderbilts, James J. Hill, August Belmont, and Thomas Fortune Ryan also challenged the metaphorical talents of progressive writers, who called these businessmen Siberian wolves, despicable despots, and bloody autocrats of monopoly. They were depicted as living in palaces, furnished with gilt doorknobs, crystal chandeliers, and other icons symbolic of their rule, from which they issued decrees ordering their private Cossacks to attack strikers, ukases raising consumer prices, and manifestos compelling business rivals to bow down to monopoly control. "Americans endure Tsars more intolerable than he of Russia," said a columnist for *Arena*, and another suspected Wall Street tycoons of plotting secretly with Nicholas, "part of a systematic and concerned effort to knit together the Princes of Privilege throughout the world."[15]

Russian-sounding terms were also applied to Americans who stood to benefit from proposed reforms. These were usually peasants, serfs, or ragged proletarians. The slums of Boston and New York were said to be worse than the meanest shacks of Tsardom. A Newark paper learned that hungry immigrants sometimes sold children for eight dollars apiece, and that a young woman had been traded to white slavers for a rooster and a chicken. "Prices are better in Russia, where daughters bring $150.00 from suppliers of Turkish harems," said the *Newark Advertiser*. Reformers in the Middle West were concerned about low farm prices and the high rate of mortgage foreclosures. They blamed the Money Tsars, bankers who connived to keep their commodity in short supply and therefore precious. These men would be wise to look at Russia, warned an agricultural writer, where hardships had driven normally conservative peasants to seek change through open rebellion. A massacre in St. Petersburg was compared with the Homestead and Pullman strikes, when American workers had been shot down by soldiers and Pinkerton detectives. Often cited were more recent skirmishes in Pennsylvania, where the most dreaded of all coal mine operators was George F. (the Russian) Baer. The St. Petersburg affair had been an ice cream social compared with the way American laboring men had been "villified, mobbed, murdered, and subjected to worse injustice than were ever the serfs of Russia, said a Seattle newspaper.[16]

America had its own pogroms, said editorialists, and these

must be stopped. One writer suggested that the Indian was "more savagely treated than the Jew in Russia." Another compared California vigilantes, whose most recent victims had been Japanese immigrants, with the Black Hundreds. Jim Crow laws protected America's own brand of serfdom, according to the *Independent,* and Russia's most stupid, bigoted, and drunken peasants could not match the conduct of Southerners at lynching bees. A race riot in Atlanta was called an American Kishinev by *Outlook,* wholly comparable in "brutality and wanton cruelty and fiendish rage and indiscriminate savagery." Tsarist evils were great enough to be all things to all people. A Nashville editor resented Northerners who insisted upon federal laws to protect Negroes in the South. Those who wanted to interfere with states' rights, he said, "would make admirable partners for the Tsar of Russia."[17]

"The political struggle that has been going on in the United states," the *Review of Reviews* explained, "is part and parcel of the same movement that has stirred up the Poles, the Finns, the Jews, and the great masses of Muscovite peasantry." Russians had been driven to violent rebellion, but this might still be avoided in the United States. "Evolution or revolution?" questioned the *World Today,* which was certain blood would flow unless bosses and monopolists changed their ways. Williams Jennings Bryan remarked with uncharacteristic subtlety, "When the people of Darkest Russia can make such progress toward American ideals, there is every reason to think that Americans can do the same."[18]

The revolutionary vocabulary of progressivism might well mislead foreigners. Exaggeration usually was no more than a device for prompting mild reforms. Russians could not know that the movement was fundamentally conservative, the pulpit more important than the soapbox in the instigation of causes appealing to a Puritan's conscience, a Victorian's obsession with moral progress, and a patriot's fear that ancient American ideals were being destroyed by modern political and industrial systems. Structural changes in the business-labor-government relationship, of the kind later associated with the 1930s, were usually considered to be undesirable. While impressive in number, reforms were in the nature of small repairs designed to patch up the American way in order to make certain that it would not break down.[19]

Indeed most Americans were horrified by the kind of changes advocated by Eugene V. Debs of the Socialist party. They feared that radicalism was on the rise. In the presidential election of 1904, Debs had received over four hundred thousand votes, a quadrupling of his strength since 1900.

In early 1905, "Big Bill" Haywood organized the Industrial Workers of the World (iww) with revolutionary programs and a membership drive so successful that Debs was said to have been extremely envious. Members of Daniel DeLeon's Socialist Labor party invaded Wall Street to pass out their "Workers Arise" leaflets. The president raved about the menace, editors published gloomy predictions of the future, and progressive leaders did not mind admitting that pet reforms, besides being moral in themselves, would have the practical effect of easing the pressures from radical reformers.

Progressives were equally selective in the foreign movements they would support. So far, however, the behavior of Russia's revolutionaries had been impeccable in the eyes of progressives. Throughout 1904 the unhappy condition of the Russian people was increasingly the subject of sermons, speeches, women's club study projects, magazine thrillers, and front-page play in papers. Newly formed committees debated various plans for reforming the Tsar's empire. Some wanted to bombard Nicholas with petitions, displaying the power of public opinion. Among petitions mailed to St. Petersburg in 1904 was one protesting the imprisonment of the celebrated writer and revolutionary, Maxim Gorky. "The American heart beats with sympathetic throb to the aspiritions of liberty-lovers throughout the world," read the petition. Russian officials considered the language insulting, and Gorky suffered for it. He hoped there would be no more petitions in his behalf.[20]

Americans also promised to send money, enough to finance a dozen revolutions. Fund-raising committees were formed by patriotic, political, and civic groups, business and church organizations, labor unions, immigrant clubs, and philanthropic societies. All set high quotas but frequently engaged in arguments over how the money was to be spent. "Books of Common Prayer should be distributed throughout Russia," an Episcopal youth group in Buffalo was told. An Indianapolis Republican club wanted to ship "millions of brochures, inciting rebellion and in the simplest of phrases instructing the masses in the operation of American democracy." Cargoes of food and medical supplies would be more useful, some suggested, while others wanted to smuggle armaments into the Romanov empire. "Crates of bombs will pay the best dividends on America's investment," an Akron businessman declared in a luncheon club speech.[21]

Other committees applied pressure to the United States government, calling upon it not to shrink from national responsibilities. Telegrams, letters, editorials, and petitions demanded numerous types of governmental action. Some said that President Roosevelt should do the job himself with a few of those oral salvos he periodically fired at rascals in one corner of the earth or another. Other suggestions were that he should call a conference of the powers and arrange a multilateral destruction of Nicholas; use his prestige to have Russia thrown out of peace conferences at The Hague; break diplomatic relations; abrogate the commercial treaty, or at the very least impose harsh trade sanctions. The United States Embassy and all consulates in Russia must serve as "fortresses in which to shield and shelter those persecuted thousands fleeing the Imperial knout," said one commentator. In addition Congress was called upon to ease immigration restrictions for refugees. All else failing, citizens urged the Navy to send battleships to Russia. A Cincinnati women's club heard a lecture, with maps, on strategic theory relative to the Gulf of Finland. During the question period that followed, it was pointed out that fourteen-inch guns lacked the range to bombard central St. Petersburg, making necessary the landing of marines and occupation of the Winter Palace. Tsarist armies could not stand long against "our young trustees of civilization," the ladies were told.[22]

American volunteers in Russia reported that stories and rumors from across the Atlantic had done much to inspire revolutionary fervor. "The glad news that American help was on the way was circulated among the multitudes," reported the *Hull House Bulletin*. Peasants, workers, and students "all fell in love with the United States," displaying "heartfelt sentiments" each time they met a representative of that country, said the *New York Herald*. Some knowledge of the benefactor was obtained from translations of dime novels, containing adventures of Nick Carter, Dick Trueblood, Buffalo Bill Cody, and other chivalric figures. At a military academy in St. Petersburg, American novelettes were passed among cadets in the manner of subversive tracts until the day they were confiscated. In their pages, smudged from extensive handling, a young Russian could read that help always arrived in the nick of time and that all was well in the end.[23]

Experienced insurrectionists were nearly as optimistic. Perhaps a few were wary of the widely accepted belief that Americans always supported revolutions, or doubted that progressivism's crusading spirit was all that it seemed to be. But only a dedicated cynic could ignore specific promises, and there had been so many of these. Revolutionary leaders packed valises and set off for America, where they planned to pick up money and work out a strategy for joint military operations.

Gapon

2. Bloody Sunday

"RUSSIAN REVOLUTION BEGINS." "Downfall of Empire Now Threatened." "Day of Reckoning at Last Arrives." Headlines were enormous on July 29, 1904, when Americans learned that Viacheslav von Plehve had been assassinated.

The infamous minister of interior had been driving through St. Petersburg on his way to deliver a report to the Tsar. On a corner waited Igor Sazonov, a university student and member of the Social Revolutionary Organization of Combat. His aim was perfect as he threw a bomb toward an open window of the passing carriage. The Cubs should hire him as a pitcher, the *Chicago News* suggested in an editorial praising Sazonov.[1]

Outside of Russia, where the murderer's party affiliation was not immediately known, there was speculation on the origins of the act. Next to Pobedonostev, Plehve had been the the most hated man in Russia. Liberals resented limitations he had recently placed upon zemstvos, which were provincial assemblies normally allowed to voice polite grievances and to go through the motions of local self-government. Urban workers had regarded Plehve as the nation's number one policeman, the executioner of strikers. Peasants remembered that he had ordered hundreds flogged to death in the country around Ekaterinoslav, and Jews recalled his instigation of the Kishinev pogrom.

New York's *Sun, Press,* and *Post* called Plehve a monster, beast, Svengali, and bloody-handed brute. "Good riddance!" they all agreed. The *Times,* more restrained, joined a number of papers that drew distinctions between good assassinations and bad ones, pointing out that Plehve had been totally unlike Lincoln, Garfield, and McKinley, who had done nothing to justify violence against them. The Russian minister was one of the few men in the world who really deserved to be murdered, the *Boston Transcript* observed. "The bomb is the only possible response of the people," the *Review of Reviews* said in explaining how Russians had been executed, exiled, and imprisoned without recourse to trial by jury. In its "Plea for Terrorism" the *Independent* encouraged Russians to do away with the entire government. Assassination, it said, was more humanitarian than general revolution in that it cost fewer lives; but, nonetheless, terrorists must be careful "not to kill innocent bystanders, if possible." The *Detroit News* was pessimistic. It criticized Russians for not having dispatched Plehve sooner and doubted that they had sufficient backbone for similar action against the Tsar. The conservative *North American Review* stated that it never condoned murder under normal circumstances but was much impressed by the fact that this one had been approved by some of Russia's most important business leaders. The *Florida Times-Union* found yet another reason to praise the deed, saying that it should prove to Americans outside the South that lynchings, while regrettable, were sometimes necessary.[2]

The assassination inspired rallies in Cincinnati, Chicago, Detroit, and New York. The *American Israelite* took pains to explain why Jews were taking part in the celebrations: they were "no doubt recent arrivals from Russia, who themselves had felt the iron hand of Plehve." The paper added that Jews in Russia generally were law-abiding and probably had not taken part in the bomb plot.[3]

The *Israelite* was aware of the growing controversy over the manner of Plehve's demise. While many Americans admired the act without reservation, others raised the issue of ends and means. A Chicago clergyman denounced the "universal delight of the American people over an immoral act." The *Nation* admitted that Plehve had been guilty of murder, but two wrongs did not make a right, "even though manufacturers and society ladies had contributed to the expense of the plot." Some editors regretted their earlier enthusiasm for revolutionaries—uneducated Russians could not after all be expected to conduct themselves properly. A certain Oriental indifference to moral responsibility made them incapable of self-government, said one commentator. A Florida editor was forced to conclude that "no people except those of Teutonic blood" were deserving of democratic rights. The *New York American* called the assassination a mistake, but only because it would harm the revolution's reputation in America: "The greatest sufferers from this crime will be the friends of liberty in Russia."[4]

Thinking wishfully, Russian ambassador Arturo Cassini spoke of an antirevolutionary tide in American public opinion. He grew careless, telling reporters of his hopes for bloody reprisals against radicals in his homeland. Reaction was immediate. There were scathing editorial attacks, threatening letters, and hostile demonstrations outside the Russian embassy. When Count Cassini asked the United States government to protect him, guards were provided by the District of Columbia police, thanks to a phone call from Secretary of State John Hay, who was more than happy to render this service. During the previous summer, shortly after the Kishinev pogrom, Hay had promised a delegation of American Jews that the government would not ignore the plight of their coreligionists in Russia. At that time he had discussed with Roosevelt the possibility of "summary action" and "going to extremes with Russia." But Plehve's murder caused Hay to change his point of view. Shocked by the assassination, he saw it as a slap at order and established social structure. He sent the usual message of condolence to the Tsar, but to Cassini spoke more earnestly than was necessary in expressing his "personal horror and sympathy."[5]

Despite controversy over the moral implications of assassination, public interest in the revolution continued to rise. A visit of the Russian cruiser *Lena* to San Francisco brought jeering crowds to the waterfront. Books by Tolstoy and Gorky sold better than ever before. A new novel about Russia, *Olive Latham,* was advertised in store windows as a romantic story of nihilism and love. The *New York Times* commented, "Public demand naturally shifts to books about the dominion of the Tsar and its storied misrule."[6]

Unlike the bombing of Plehve, which had required strained justifications, events of the next few months were received with unqualified joy by the revolution's American sympathizers.

The Tsar's government failed to react as would be expected to the assassination. Instead of mass arrests and punishments, censorship was temporarily relaxed and manifestos were issued that proclaimed the affection Nicholas felt for his subjects. Moderation on the part of the government resulted more from fear than love, due to recent reports of Japanese victories, army mutinies, and revolutionary agitation throughout the empire. The Tsar was forced to choose a political moderate, Prince Peter Svyatopolk-Mirsky, to succeed Plehve as the minister of interior. The atmosphere was highly promising in the view of zemstvo leaders who decided to meet in St. Petersburg and draw up a petition for reforms. Prince Mirsky objected, but the liberals convened anyway.

Police gave them no trouble. The petition framed by the ninety-eight country gentlemen startled the government, for it contained requests for full civil liberties as well as for a representative national assembly.

"Situation Most Remarkable in Russia's History," the *Providence Daily Journal* proclaimed in a headline. American papers and magazines heaped praise upon the wise and courageous men who had met in St. Petersburg—liberals had set the revolution on the right track; now Russia had its own founding fathers, who would soon create a congress and a bill of rights. Editors confessed that the Plehve affair had made them doubt the rightness of the cause, but all doubts had vanished thanks to the zemstvo leaders, described as proprietors, landowners who understood the rights of property, conservatives, members of the upper middle class, and the thinking elements of the nation. "They are not members of revolutionary societies," the *Review of Reviews* said, "but are substantial citizens."[7]

Nicholas did not agree. Following ministerial consultation, he decided that the petitioners had been impertinent. As zemstvo leaders they had been permitted to comment on affairs in their own localities, but they had no business making suggestions that concerned the national government. The Tsar's prestige could allow not the slightest implication that he had been forced to make concessions. Instead, Nicholas announced, he himself would grant reforms, through arbitrary decision, prompted solely by paternal concern for his people. He issued a decree on Christmas Day that listed several benign acts the government would consider in the future, but emphasized that autocratic rule would continue and absolutely forbade further revolutionary agitation.

A few American opinion-makers congratulated Nicholas. From now on, the *Nation* stated, Russian troubles must be blamed on overzealous reformers and not on the Tsar. The *Chicago Evening Post* spoke highly of "the response of a benevolent despot to the cry of his people"—the Little Father loved his subjects even if conditions prevented him from doing much for them; he also loved his wife and children, liked to putter in the garden, and played an excellent game of croquet. Such a man could not be all bad.[8]

A much larger number of publications considered the decree to be a defeat for liberal aspirations. They said that the Tsar remained a tyrant and a hypocrite, a liar who had no intention of keeping his promises. He was called sly and slimy, spineless, a jellyfish of first rank, unmanly, a pathetic creature not more than five feet in height—"He must peer up to see the eyes of a woman."[9]

Zemstvo leaders were well aware that they had been defeated. None believed the Tsar's vague references to future reforms. The more timid among them returned to their country provinces, while others remained in the capital and formed the Union of Emancipation, an organization willing to work with SRs and SDs. Liaison was also established with the professional unions recently created by lawyers, authors, professors, journalists, doctors, and engineers. An abundance of leaders sought enough followers to start the mass upheaval now thought to be necessary. Pamphlets and speeches reached new levels of ferocity, but results were small. Activists cursed the docile, long-suffering nature of their countrymen, as well as the biting cold that kept people off the streets and made January an unlikely month for revolution.

American journalists were equally impatient with the Russians. It was well known that the revolution had begun many months before, on July 28 to be precise: Did revolutionaries understand this? Why didn't they do something? "Americans were fearless when they threw off their chains in Seventy-Six," said the *Newark Daily Advertiser*, "but Russians evidently do not have what it takes."[10]

Revolutionaries were wondering what they could do to get something started when the Russian government, through an incredible blunder, solved the problem for them.

George Gapon, priest and liberal of sorts, had formed an Association of Factory Workers in St. Petersburg. Talking insistently of his humility and loyalty, Father Gapon was proud that his organization included few radicals, and equally proud that it was sponsored by the police department. (The government was more than glad to encourage workmen to follow priests instead of Social Democrats.) Gapon had faith in the Tsar. He believed that Nicholas was at heart a benevolent man who did not know the truth about conditions in Russia because of lies his ministers told him. He was certain that once Nicholas knew the real facts, he would grant reforms without delay. The priest sat down to write a petition that he thought would surely bring tears to the eyes of the Little Father in the Winter Palace. He begged for constitutional monarchy, liberty of speech and press, judicial and tax reforms, universal education, and the right of labor to organize. Gapon stressed the loyalty of the workers he represented. They demanded nothing; they only prayed that their sovereign would condescend to read their petition and consider it. "Two roads alone are open to us," the petition read. "One leads to freedom and happiness, the other to the grave. Tell us upon which we are to travel, Sire; we will follow it without a murmur, even though it be the way of death."[11]

The priest announced that a delegation of several thousand workers would deliver the document to the palace on Sunday, January 22. Nicholas, who could not decide what to do, departed from St. Petersburg after placing the problem in the hands of his uncle, the Grand Duke Vladimir.

Gapon prepared the ceremony with great care. Workers were to wear their Sunday clothes and carry hats in hands as they approached the palace. They would carry icons and portraits of the Tsar, and slogans on placards must be either religious or patriotic. They would sing the national anthem as they marched. It would be helpful too, Gapon stressed, if workers brought their most appealing children, preferably gaunt and sad of eye, to the head of the column.

The parade moved slowly through the broad avenues. History contains many sentimental descriptions of an off-key "God Save the Tsar," the frosty breaths, the squeak of thousands of boots on packed snow, and marchers who slipped and fell on icy streetcar tracks. Ranks of soldiers barred entry to Palace Square. Leaders of the procession halted, bracing themselves against pressure at their backs. If an order to disperse was given, no one heard it. Most of the marchers had never heard machine gun fire, and those farther to the rear thought snare drums were being played. The more emphatic sound of rifle volleys made them turn and run. According to moderate estimates, about five hundred were killed and three thousand wounded.

Father Gapon, playing dead among the bodies, almost froze before darkness enabled him to make his way back to association headquarters in the Putilov Iron Works. Expecting arrest, he hastily wrote another document: "There is no Tsar. . . . It is high time for the Russian workman to begin without him to carry on the struggle for national freedom. You have my blessing for the cause. Tomorrow I will be among you."[12] Aided by a disguise, he slipped out of the city that night and a few days later was safely out of the country.

Manifestos poured from the headquarters of zemstvos, professional unions, srs, and sds. This time the people of Russia listened. Strikes and riots broke out in every corner of the empire, and assassinations of bureaucrats were reported from every province. In some regions of Finland and Poland the death rate was so high that government ceased to function. srs bombed the wrong uncle of the Tsar. The intended victim was the Grand Duke Vladimir, who had ordered the massacre, but the Grand Duke Sergius was killed instead. St. Petersburg University students ripped to shreds a full-length painting of Nicholas. A New York newspaperman joined the scramble for pieces of the canvas. He wanted the Tsar's face but had to settle for a bit of sleeve, which he mailed back to his paper for reproduction.[13]

The government retaliated. It tried the pogrom device a number of times during February, but found it increasingly difficult to control the hatred of revolutionaries. Police and soldiers shot thousands of troublemakers. Entire towns were burned in Armenia. The Holy Synod blessed all the faithful and warned them not to participate in strikes: "Work, according to God's word, with the sweat of your brow, and remember that he who will not work, neither shall he eat. Beware of false counsellors who, pretending anxiety over your needs and well-being, foment disorders which lose you your homes and your food." The Tsar returned to the palace. He seemed perplexed, questioning the wisdom of the massacre no matter how carefully ministers explained that it was sometimes necessary to teach lessons that would be remembered. At last ministers were forced to select certain Putilov workers, instruct them, and take them to see Nicholas. They fell to their knees and begged forgiveness for having taken part in Gapon's march. They had been in the wrong, they said, and the government had been justified in firing upon them. The emperor's face brightened at these words. He fed his guests tea and cakes and gave them a fatherly lecture on good citizenship.[14]

While they feared the current mood of the population, the Tsar's ministers believed that "the main effect produced Sunday was outside Russia, rather than inside." Gapon's meek-sounding petition had been "one of those grandiloquent products of propaganda . . . with which our revolutionists [are] habitually endeavoring to enlist the sympathies of public opinion abroad in their warfare against the government of their own country."[15]

Bloody Sunday, as it was called everywhere, inaugurated America's period of wildest infatuation with the Russian revolution. Father Gapon was acceptable as a hero: no radicalism had stained his motives; his marchers had displayed perfect manners (all they had wanted were rights such as those enjoyed in America). In spite of this, an outraged press declared, they had been butchered; slaughtered in cold blood; shot down like dogs, in a frightful carnage, a hideous massacre, a wholesale murder of innocents. Forty thousand had died, or fifty thousand, or a hundred thousand, according to press reports. Few correspondents passed up the chance to describe blood on the snow, pretty girls raped by Cossacks, wounded children crying, worshipers slain in churches, and patients murdered in their hospital beds. "Like the victims of the Boston Massacre, the martyred workmen of St. Petersburg have not died in vain, one editor said; and another wrote, "The spirit of Patrick Henry is abroad in the land of the Tsar."[16]

It was difficult for newsmen to find fresh superlatives for Nicholas, variously described as a reincarnation of Ivan the Terrible, the rottenest Romanov of all time, history's greatest murderer, monstrous moron, and semi-idiot. He had "no virtues at all," said one writer. Lincoln Steffens wrote an open letter to the Tsar more violent than any of his muckraking articles. Mark Twain compared the royal family to a nest of cobras. He wished somebody would assassinate them, and said, "so does every sane person in the world—but who has the grit to say so?"[17]

Boisterous demonstrations in several cities led to injuries and arrests, and two Cincinnati women were hospitalized following a stampede to buy newspapers that headlined the massacre. New Yorkers bought tickets at scalpers' prices for Bartley Campbell's melodrama, *Siberia*. "They shouted 'Death to the Tsar' until the building rocked," reported the *New York Times*. Buffalo Bill Cody announced that he was dropping the Cossack Extravaganza from his Wild West Show. Students hissed whenever Nicholas was mentioned in lectures at the University of Chicago, and church congregations applauded sermons vividly describing the tortures awaiting him in Hell. The *New York Times*, which regularly printed contributions from amateur poets, could not cope with the "amazingly heavy rain of impassioned verse about the Tsar."[18]

Ambassador Cassini refused to talk with the newsmen who asked him for statements. He knew that a segment of the press had been calling for his ejection from the United States. In "great anguish of mind" over present trends in public opinion, he knew that he would have to take some kind of action. In an article for the *World Today* Cassini asked for better Russian-American understanding and revealed what he considered to be the true facts about Bloody Sunday. According to Cassini, rowdies, drunks, and socialists had caused the trouble, besieging the palace and placing in jeopardy the lives of those inside. Soldiers had been forced to shoot in self-defense, he said. The *World Today,* immediately under attack for having printed outlandish lies, joined other publications in demanding Cassini's recall.[19]

Secretary of State Hay did not know what to think about Bloody Sunday. Messages to him from Robert S. McCormick, ambassador in St. Petersburg, said that Gapon probably was a dangerous man who had meant to seize the Tsar and hold him hostage. Moreover, McCormick stated, the soldiers had been "invariably polite in their admonitions to the crowd" before commencing firing. On the other hand, the ambassador said that he had personally inspected Gapon's men and found that "they had not the look of revolutionists." Admitting he was in a quandary, McCormick concluded that socialist agitators, scattered among an otherwise peaceful crowd, probably had yelled things which forced the troops to fire. Of one thing he felt sure. Reporters were criminally exaggerating the incident, and he feared the effect upon public opinion. "Please do not be too impulsive," he said to an American correspondent. "You do not have to succumb too greatly to impressions of scenes you witnessed yesterday and send too vivid a description."[20]

Other members of Roosevelt's administration revealed

similar worries. They feared that there might be more Bloody Sundays, giving the press further opportunities for sensational reporting. As the *Saturday Evening Post* said, "All this denunciation of Russian [rule] in every city, town, village, and hamlet of the United States ought to be exceedingly valuable to the revolution." The *Post* was glad that public opinion was "so much more powerful than it used to be."[21]

During most of the nineteenth century the government had been able to resist pressures from zealous reformers, applying strategic thought to popular humanitarian instincts. But more recently, in 1898, war had resulted from journalistic determination and a president's anxieties over his popularity with voters.

Miliukov

3. Wild to Go to Russia

THE INTERNAL CRISIS that followed Bloody Sunday brought an end to official moderation and to the career of Prince Mirsky. Now in command at the Ministry of Interior, with the title Imperial Chief of Police, was General Dmitri Trepov, who referred to himself as the strong right arm of the Tsar. It was Trepov who ordered February massacres in Finland, Poland, and Armenia. He conducted pogroms with special zeal, for he strongly suspected that Jews had fomented all of Russia's troubles. He thought that Father Gapon, for example, had been the unwitting pawn in a Hebrew plot. There was no evidence, of course, for Jews were notoriously cunning and devious in their schemes, but Trepov trusted his policeman's instinct in such matters. He was certain that the anti-Christs had subsidized Gapon, probably with funds obtained through their connections in the United States. America was another subject which aggravated the general. He never doubted his ability to crush unarmed peasants and factory hands, but was said to worry about those restless people across the Atlantic and their vigorous promises to Russian subversives. That which worried Trepov delighted his enemies. Liberals looked to "sincere friends in the United States," and socialists counted upon "American comrades."[1]

Carrying a strapped valise and a bottle of Mothersill's Seasick Remedy, Paul Miliukov entered New York harbor in early December 1904. Dutifully, he praised the skyscrapers of lower Manhattan for the benefit of reporters who had come aboard to ask how he liked the United States. Journalists knew they were interviewing a famous man. Articles on important revolutionary leaders usually had favored either Miliukov or Maxim Gorky. While Gorky undoubtedly was the better known, some Americans were bothered by his socialist leanings. Miliukov had no such handicap. When the history professor had lectured at the University of Chicago in 1903, the press had approved of his moderate revolutionary ideas and publicized him as most prominent among all Russian liberals. Now he was called the George Washington of current events, a gallant fighter for freedom and future president of a republican Russia.[2]

Miliukov drew respectful ovations when he spoke in Boston, New York, and other cities. Not a flamboyant orator, he often apologized for his scholarly manner and habit of referring to uninteresting details of Russian history. Not until late January did applause turn to cheers. Miliukov modestly attributed his sudden popularity to the effects of Bloody Sunday, but success also stemmed from his use of new lecture techniques. In rave reviews, the press noted that he had dropped his intellectual approach, spoke more powerfully, and got right to the point. He flattered Americans on skyscrapers and water closets, on military might and Christian humanitarianism. He freely admitted that most of his own inspiration had come from American history, especially the Revolution; the Constitution; Washington and Lincoln; and the Winning of the West, which he compared to Siberia, still a wilderness due to government restrictions on private initiative. Russians, he said, were fundamentally democratic, individualistic, and loving of their fellow men. They were just like Americans, and would prove it if only given the chance. But odds were against them, said Miliukov. Anecdotes on Cossack cruelties became more graphic with every speech, as he emphasized that victims included numerous small businessmen and demure female students. He denounced all radicals and apologized for a few isolated instances of mob violence and assassination.

Miliukov's pragmatism was oddly limited. Having achieved celebrity status, he dismayed American sponsors by refusing to participate in fund-raising drives. On a visit to New York's lower East Side, a center of interest in Russian affairs, he disappointed social worker Lillian Wald by showing contempt for people who were working for the revolution in practical ways. He was described as bored, gloomy, and concerned about self-respect. He explained, without much enthusiasm, that his appeal was not to America's pocketbook but to its mind.

Seeking tangible profits, other Russians headed for the East Side after leaving their ships. There they were certain they would find all the help they needed for their programs. The Ninth District was described by its congressman as: "the home of the tenements, push-carts, paupers, and tuberculosis. It is the experimental laboratory of the sentimental settlement worker, the horrible example of the pious moralist, and the chosen prey of the smug philanthropist. Geographically it is located in the slums; industrially it belongs to the sweat-shop system; politically it is a dependency of Tammany Hall." Over two hundred thousand refugees from pogroms had found their way to the lower East Side. Among institutions they had brought to America were political parties—SD, SR, and *Bund*, all dedicated to raising money and arousing American opinion against the Tsar.[3]

Difficulties were tremendous for the Russian visitors. With no subtle Miliukovs to guide them, propagandists turned out manifestos so shrill and violent as to frighten prospective contributors. Little help came from the native-born comrades, who followed Debs and DeLeon. Now and then American socialists offered suggestions and lent a hand with the folding chairs at Clinton Hall, but most were inclined to be snobbish, and the odors of the Ninth District were clearly annoying to them. Nor did the Jewish *Bund* receive much comfort from nonimmigrant brethren. Respectable Jews disowned greenhorn efforts to raise money for the purpose of smuggling guns into Russia. According to B'nai B'rith, pogroms should be opposed only by "the employment of moral force." In addition, there were handicaps of a kind faced by all new arrivals—problems of language, uncertainties over how to dress, and a pathetic ignorance of that world to which they must appeal outside the tenement district. One young SD, ordered to attend to some party business in Chicago, was defeated by the streetcar transfer system long before he reached Grand Central Station.[4]

But the visitors found certain advantages too, the greatest being America's current entrancement by the revolution—a warm, hazy glow that obscured normal political differences. Russians found valuable friends in the settlement houses of the East Side. Lillian Wald, who managed the Henry Street Settlement House, was at first wary of revolutionary agitators in the neighborhood. Her doubts were overcome by "a long procession of saints and martyrs," who came to tea and taught her to see "in the gigantic struggle in Russia a world movement for freedom and progress that is our struggle too." Miss Wald threw herself into committee-making and money-raising. When shaggy envoys appeared, she provided them with hair-cuts and presentable clothes, sponsored their first speeches, introduced them to journalists, and made travel arrangements for their forays out of the East Side. Thanks to Miss Wald's connections, touring revolutionaries received similar assistance from Jane Addams of Chicago's Hull House and Helena S. Dudley of Boston's Denison House.[5]

Another center of hospitality was University Settlement, headquarters for a group of young New Yorkers who called themselves gentlemen socialists. Sons of wealthy families— William English Walling, Ernest Poole, James Phelps-Stokes, Gaylord Wilshire, Arthur Bullard, Kellogg Durland, and others—spent many a convivial hour at the Little Hungary Café, located not far from the settlement house. There they drank wine from shaving mugs, sang Russian songs, and flirted with the refugee girls. Mainly they talked about "reforms and revolutions of diverse kinds." Their work at University Settlement was important, but dull compared with the great struggle to overthrow Tsarist tyranny. They were "wild to go to Russia," Ernest Poole said.[6]

In the regions beyond the slums were the committees, formed in cities everywhere by Americans of all types, waiting to greet picturesque visitors. The most powerful of these groups, the Friends of Russian Freedom, was headed by William Dudley Foulke, eminent Republican from Indiana. Among active members were George Kennan, Mark Twain, the Rev. Minot J. Savage, William Dean Howells, Alice Stone Blackwell, and Julia Ward Howe. The Friends worked in conjunction with the settlement houses and East Side revolutionary parties, despite occasional bickering over which group would be first to sponsor speeches by the most famous refugees. This honor usually went to the Friends, because of nationwide connections, superior influence with the press, and the enviable ease with which they were able to arrange banquets in the best hotels.

The press kept track of over forty Russians who toured the country in the early months of 1905. Alexander Petrunkevich stressed liberalism and personal friendship with Miliukov, but political distinctions were not at this time important to American audiences. *Bundists* Arcady Kremer and Ezra Berg, who had been playing the lecture circuit for two years, were amazed by the cheers they received after Bloody Sunday. A team of SRs, billed simply as Nicolaev & Rosenbaum, thrilled listeners with inside stories of assassinations they had arranged. Isador Ladov specialized in "Experiences of an Exile in Siberia," and another Social Revolutionary, Chaim Zhitlowsky, described Tsarist atrocities so effectively that women sobbed and screamed. Gregor Uriev had brought several Social Democrats to the United States, but they failed to establish useful connections and remained in the East Side.[7]

The celebrated actors Paul Orlenev and Mme. Alla Nazimova arrived in New York with an entire theatrical company. They planned to put on plays of social protest by Tolstoy, Gorky, and Gogol. After a few performances before Third Avenue audiences, they were discovered by some Astor and Vanderbilt wives, who arranged special benefit appearances for them. Orlenev prospered. He opened his own theater, Orlenev's Lyceum, and became, according to the *Saturday Evening Post,* "the most romantic figure in the theatrical life of New York."[8]

Among SRs in Russia was a personality who would, revolutionaries believed, almost certainly capture the heart of America if she could survive the journey there. Catherine Breshkovsky was a white-haired grandmother who had spent eight years in a St. Petersburg prison and another fourteen in Siberian exile. A woman of excellent family (Americans were told she was the daughter of nobility), Mme. Breshkovsky had lost her early faith in liberalism and turned to terrorism as the only hope for change. The SRs decided to export these attractions, but were perhaps unwise in their choice of an American sponsor—the renowned anarchist, Emma Goldman. It was felt that the two women, holding similar political views, would work well together. Miss Goldman, who had dedicated her life to anarchy, was notorious as the mastermind behind the 1892 plot to assassinate steel tycoon Henry Clay Frick. Although both shot and stabbed, he had survived. Faced with new responsibilities, Miss Goldman feared that she might fail again. Besides, as she told

SR emissaries Nicolaev & Rosenbaum, her connection with Breshkovsky's tour would do it more harm than good. Miss Goldman certainly could not imagine that the respectable Friends of Russian Freedom would want anything to do with one of her projects. Nevertheless she promised to try and began with a letter to Alice Stone Blackwell, the Boston philanthropist who had once admired some Goldman poetry.[9]

She was surprised one day by a visit from Mrs. Blackwell and William Dudley Foulke, national president of the Friends. Both were excited about the Breshkovsky idea, and plans were developed in perfect harmony. "Imagine," the anarchist wrote later, "the good Rooseveltian Republican in Emma Goldman's flat at 210 East Thirteenth Street, sipping tea and discussing ways and means to undermine the Russian autocracy." For the sake of the cause Miss Goldman had disguised her true identity, and Mrs. Blackwell had not given her away.[10]

The Grandmother of the Revolution, as Mme. Breshkovsky was billed, received a noisy welcome on the East Side. At one reception people wept, sang "The Marseillaise," and carried her on their shoulders. Their guest was described as a nervous woman who smoked cigarettes endlessly, and who was clearly relieved when Miss Goldman effected an escape to the House on Henry Street. Lillian Wald wrote: "Who of those that sat around the fire with her in the sitting room . . . can ever forget the experience? After two decades of prison and Siberian exile, she sat with us and thrilled us with glimpses of the courage of those who had answered the call." When Breshkovsky visited University Settlement, the gentlemen socialists were "struck with awe by her blood-curdling adventures," and wanted to leave for Russia at the earliest possible moment. Luncheon with Julia Ward Howe produced a minor fiasco. The authoress of "Battle Hymn of the Republic," now a hazy eighty-six years old, had planned to honor her guest by playing some Russian music on the piano. Breshkovsky emitted a "cry of horror" when she heard the strains of "God Save the Tsar." But her first formal address at Clinton Hall was a rousing success except for the loss of her sponsor. Emma Goldman was the most dangerous woman in America, noted one paper in explaining why the police had hauled her off to jail.[11]

Bloody Sunday turned Breshkovsky into a national celebrity. Articles appeared in major magazines, and invitations arrived from city councils, lodges, and businessmen's luncheon clubs. Breshkovsky advanced beyond the tenement district, appearing at New York's Sunrise Club and Cooper Union before enthusiastic audiences of thousands. Then it was on to Chicago, where Comrade Peter Sissman escorted her to socialist functions on the South Side. A goodly sum was collected, reported the *Social Democratic Herald*. Eventually Breshkovsky was claimed by more respectable elements, represented by Jane Addams and Judge Edward Brown, who guided her north. Opera singers adorned her appearance at the Auditorium, and matrons of Lake Shore Drive contended for her presence in their drawing rooms. "She painted a picture so horrible that the women were shocked," commented one editor. New committees were formed. "Chicago Society Women Will Aid Russian Revolt," announced a headline in the *Chicago American*. Experiences were similar in Detroit and Buffalo. Boston papers spoke of deafening roars of welcome in Faneuil Hall, and Wellesley girls were said to have responded hysterically to the grimmer Siberian anecdotes. In Philadelphia, chanting demonstrators carried a terrified old woman on their shoulders for nearly an hour.[12]

Returning to New York, Breshkovsky said that she wished to return immediately to Russia. She gave the ten thousand dollars she had collected to a Norwegian sailor, who promised to use it to smuggle guns into Odessa. She expressed gratitude for the immensity of her welcome, but, like other touring comrades, was disappointed over the amount of money collected. Most revolutionaries were confident, however, that

America's financial response would improve during the months ahead. Upon returning to Russia, they told of their warm reception in the United States and urged the revolution's most glorious heroes to make similar journeys. Some said that even Maxim Gorky might be persuaded to travel to the United States.[13]

Because some Americans wanted to give more than money and to enjoy the adventure of a trip to Russia, revolutionaries did not lack for lively companionship during the voyage home. An Associated Press story said that dozens of young Philadelphians were leaving for the struggle and that there were "scores like them all over the United States." According to a concerned Russian bureaucrat, Baron Vladimir von Freisen, twenty-six American ruffians had met in New Orleans and drawn straws to determine who would be the Tsar's assassin. He said they had taken "an oath of secrecy and disappeared into the night."[14]

William Jennings Bryan was an adventurer who craved publicity. Believing that too many voters considered him a country bumpkin, Bryan had decided to build a new reputation as an international trouble shooter, "standing up to foreigners," as he put it. Traveling at rapid speed, throughout Europe, Asia, and Africa, he scolded the British for being imperialistic, the French for exhibiting nude paintings in the Louvre, the Egyptians because they had not repaired the Sphinx, and the Chinese for inattention to Christian missionaries. His plan in Russia involved nothing more violent than to give the Tsar a good talking-to and thereby improve his own chances in the next presidential election. He confronted Nicholas II in both 1904 and 1906, standing up to the Tsar on such matters as temperance, protestantism, and American democratic principles. He suggested that Leo Tolstoy's Doctrine of Love be instituted throughout all of Russia. The Tsar found his guest "quaint," but Tolstoy was embarrassed, saying, "Bryan certainly does talk a lot." Most of this talk was recorded, word for word, in the papers of the Middle West, where Bryan received a hero's welcome after each of his missions abroad. He heard himself introduced as America's Lancelot and wept without shame whenever an audience sang his favorite hymn, "I'll Go Where You Want Me To Go, Dear Lord."[15]

The gentlemen socialists of University Settlement attended farewell parties and made sailing arrangements on fashionable White Star liners. Ernest Poole said that the speeches of Catherine Breshkovsky had made him decide to go to Russia, while Kellogg Durland and Arthur Bullard designated Bloody Sunday as the source of their inspiration. Howard Brubaker credited the fire and zeal of William English Walling, saying, "He turned us all into hot revolutionists whether we were from New York, Chicago, Philadelphia, or, like myself, fresh from Indiana cornfields." Walling had several reasons for wanting to go to Russia. There he could do research for magazine articles on the nobility of the revolution and urge its leaders to travel to America and tell their story. He was sure that both types of activity would boost money drives and also aid American socialism, which would "draw inspiration and spirit from the depth and breadth of self-sacrifice of the Russian revolutionists."[16]

On a February night in 1905, Poole celebrated at a last farewell party in the Little Hungary Café. Settlement friends were there, and Mark Twain dropped in to wish good fortune to the adventurer. They spent the night drinking, singing, and discussing the poetry of Lord Byron. The party shifted to the White Star docks shortly before ten the next morning, whereupon Poole staggered up the gangway carrying several rolls of paper to throw down on his friends. Then he slept for a day and a half.[17]

Poole liked Paris instantly and remained there for several weeks. He toured sites of historical and literary interest and also established contact with some Russians. Practicing espionage techniques, he left notes for his new acquaintances between pages of books in the National Library, studied code, and held a secret midnight rendezvous at a Latin Quarter bistro. He was delighted when a Russian gave him ciphers to deliver to revolutionaries in St. Petersburg. Poole was "crazy to get over there," he said. Passing through Berlin, he stopped only long enough to buy a fur coat and some brass knuckles. He arrived in St. Petersburg disguised as a shoe salesman.[18]

He was surprised to find Samuel S. McClure, the noted magazine publisher, in the lobby of his hotel. Poole revealed his true identity, and a gloomy conversation ensued. McClure had planned a series of articles on the revolution but now feared that it was quieting down. Poole agreed that little was happening but gave assurances that there was "human dynamite beneath the calm surface." That night he began his first free-lance magazine article: "This is a city of silent chaos." But chaos remained difficult to discover. Certainly it did not exist in the chandeliered splendor of St. Petersburg's best hotel. Fortunately, Poole met a correspondent for the *Manchester Guardian* who promised to introduce him to some revolutionaries. They struck out from the hotel, visiting illegal printing plants and odorous flats that turned Poole's stomach. He met SDs, SRs, and liberals, and all gave him conflicting versions of revolutionary goals. Poole was depressed by the absence of clean-cut issues. For political factions and their wrangling he had "very little use—what took hold of me so hard was the common purpose behind it all, to set a great people free from the tyranny that bound them down."[19]

Seeking the overall picture, Poole traveled throughout Russia and filled several notebooks with what he saw from train windows. During a Moscow stopover he was struck by contrasts between the barrack-style slums of the industrial suburbs and the beauty of the central city, with its tree-lined avenues and heavily ornamented mansions. Scorning merchants and noblemen who dwelled in such luxury, he wrote admiringly of life in the slums. He was most authoritative, however, in articles about what he called "hilarious little cafés" near Moscow University. Following unforeseen delays, Poole left for the Ukraine, where he visited farms and factories disguised as Harold McCormick, son of the American ambassador. Officials welcomed him and approved all sightseeing tours.[20]

Policemen in Armenia were not so cordial, due to the increasingly clandestine nature of the young American's activities. Poole described himself as a legendary figure among peasants, who had already heard of his travels through the underground mail. He went from village to village, viewing sites of government atrocities and vowing over and over again that America would never desert the Russian people. "Their eyes grew moist," he said of the peasants who listened to his talk of American support. He was invited to a secret meeting of munitions smugglers and attended a railroad strike, where he took photographs of Cossacks in action. Increasing attention from the police convinced Poole that he should not extend his two-month journey through Russia, and early summer found him climbing the Swiss Alps with Walling and Bullard the most recent arrivals from University Settlement. Poole later wrote, "Walking together we talked . . . of the plans and dreams we shared for the freedom of the whole human race from tyranny of every kind, from poverty and sweated toil."[21]

Following a vacation on the Dalmatian coast, Walling and Bullard reached St. Petersburg in November 1905. Bullard, who hoped to sell eyewitness stories to *Collier's* and *Harper's*, said he wanted to "go into the thick of it—try to see executions, and talk to the most desperate revolutionaries." (Later, at home, he proudly displayed a bullet hole in his straw hat, received in a skirmish not far from the Winter Palace.) Walling said he had no interest in "bullets, barricades, or conspiracies. . . . Not because I am afraid or because I don't think it worthwhile, but because my work is other—bigger and more interesting. I am trying to understand the Master Minds and Forces of the Revolution." He said he feared only "the dangers of too much hospitality. . . . The revolutionaries tell me what they will tell no one else. . . . I saw the Ministers of War and Finance for long, intimate talks last week. . . . I am every day with some prince or minister." In accounts of his tours of the provinces, he said he was "everywhere received with open arms" but once in Saratov "had to put up at a second-best hotel." In the evenings, he said, he stopped by cafés and did what he could "to inspire the socialist forces of the revolution." On a train Walling was attracted to "two charming Moscow girls, evidently of good family. . . . There are pleasant incidents like this every day," he reported. But he felt that one thing was missing to make this "the most exciting adventure a fellow ever had"—the woman he loved. He sent a cable to Anna Strunsky in San Francisco and asked her to meet him in St. Petersburg. He had little hope that she would answer his cable, much less agree to come to Russia. He assumed that "she was entirely absorbed in another man, a fine fellow whom I also know—frankly and in confidence, Jack London."22

In San Francisco some two years earlier, while London and Anna Strunsky were collaborating on a novel, they had held hands and engaged in other small displays of affection that had caused talk among the socialist elite. But the romance had not lasted because Anna had frowned on London's rough speech and crude table manners. She had felt more at ease with young men such as Walling, whom she had met during a trip to New York. As a socialist, she had deplored the materialism which flawed the novelist's political philosophy. Trying to have it both ways, London had often argued with her that the best way to show up capitalists was for a socialist to beat them at making money. He saw himself as a supersocialist, climbing to the top by his own individual efforts and dragging the masses with him. Anna, who could not abide revisionism, had told him he could not love

Karl Marx and Horatio Alger at the same time. She saw little of him thereafter and was horrified to learn, in 1904, that she had been named as corespondent in Mrs. London's divorce suit. Even without this undeserved humiliation (London's wife had confused her with another woman), Anna had been repelled by the spectacle the author was making of himself while working in behalf of the Russian revolution.[23]

Inspired by Bloody Sunday, London embarked upon a speaking tour of California schools and business clubs. His *Call of the Wild* was currently a best seller, and he drew large audiences. His message was perplexing, emphasizing the yellow peril, which he had come to fear during recent adventures in Manchuria as a war correspondent. Unless the Tsar defeated Japan, he warned, the latter would pose a dangerous threat to the United States. Urging students to go to Russia to fight for the revolution and for socialism, he said: "University men and women, you men and women in the full glory of life, here is a cause that appeals to all the romance in you. Awake to its call." Question periods after lectures produced awkward moments for London. He was challenged with such questions as, If the Tsar defeated Japan, what would happen to the revolution? London declared: "What the devil! I am first of all a white man and only then a Socialist." Equally annoying to socialists in his audiences were London's flowered cravats, goldheaded walking stick, and the Korean valet who followed him everywhere.[24]

Anna Strunsky's disenchantment with London knew no limits. Walling was overjoyed when she arrived in St. Petersburg only a few weeks after he had sent his invitation. In a café frequented by revolutionaries "a pair of hands touched, then clasped, beneath the table." Anna was an asset to Walling's group, which had also been joined by Kellogg Durland and an English photographer named Farnsworth. A proud Walling reported that all Russians, whether they were policemen or comrades, found his companion winsome and charming. A talented writer, she was able to help with the articles

Walling was writing for *American Workman, Independent,* and *Atlantic Monthly,* all concerned with the imminent doom of the ruling class throughout the world. In letters to his parents Walling revealed his gentler side, describing what it was like to be in love with the prettiest girl in the world, walking hand in hand through "a real crackerjack of a revolution . . . the time of my life, everything I have ever dreamed of." During a summer vacation in Paris, Anna and Walling were married, then returned to their work in St. Petersburg.[25]

Despite their frolics, Walling and his associates were accomplishing the goals they had set for themselves. By mid-1906, over forty of their articles, portraying the struggle against Tsarism in the most attractive terms, appeared in American magazines. And throughout Russia they were planting seeds of hope, telling revolutionaries to look to the United States for the strong helping hand that would pull them through to victory. Maxim Gorky was one who listened to the young Americans. Sitting at a table in one of the ubiquitous cafés, the renowned writer contemplated his vodka, finally agreed to travel to America, then touched his glass to those thrust out in his direction. His tour of the United States, Walling asserted, would be a smashing success. It would fill the revolutionary treasury and mean the difference between defeat and triumph.[26]

The travelers returned home in 1906. Their reactions to their journey can perhaps be summed up by those of Poole: "My trip had been a glamorous adventure into a Russia wild, strange, and deep, to write stories of its struggle for freedom and so get American aid, and then to come back to my own safe home."[27]

If Gorky had come to the United States in the Spring of 1905, his tour might have fulfilled even Walling's hopes. During this period there was no indication that the public's latest infatuation could be anything but enduring. "Americans are faithful to their principles," the *Christian Observer* said. "They will see the revolution through to its glorious conclusion."[28]

On March 4, newspapers reported another case of Tsarist treachery. Perturbed over General Trepov's failure to subdue rebellion by force, Russian ministers of state decided upon another conciliatory gesture. Nicholas announced that he was preparing a parliamentary system to be known as a Duma. This body would be consultive and have no legislative powers. Election laws would be designed to give dominant influence to "the most worthy persons," and that fundamental verity, the power of the Tsar to make arbitrary decisions based upon divine right, was not to be altered in any way. Conservative revolutionists saw the plan as a step forward. They renounced their recent support of terrorism, and Russia entered that period of relative calm about which Poole and McClure had complained at their meeting in St. Petersburg.

American journalists were not fooled by the Duma plan, which they called deceitful, hocus-pocus, a booby trap, and a sleight of hand maneuver aimed at stalling revolution until the Japanese war was over. The *Hartford Daily Courant* advised Russians not to put away their bombs too soon, and the *Kansas City Star* would accept nothing less than complete liberty. Particularly obnoxious to the *Nation* had been the Tsar's reference to divine right, "a statement more depressing, more inept, it would be hard to find in all the annals of royal blundering." Besides, as a Florida paper noted, America, not Russia, was God's country. Nor was the emperor admired for having labeled his scheme a parliamentary system. "Government modelled on the American . . . pattern is needed," the *Nation* said. A Chicago manufacturer of player pianos donated two dozen rolls of "Columbia, the Gem of the Ocean" for distribution in Russia.[29]

On Easter the Tsar decreed religious freedom for all Russians except Jews. Enhanced by pogroms in well-chosen sites, this reform further smoothed the temper of the Russian people. With the exception of papers such as the *New York Herald* (which had found that anti-Semitism was good for circulation) and William Jennings Bryan's *Commoner* (which rejoiced in behalf of Russia's Baptists), the American press was enraged. Horrors were catalogued in stories headlined: "Massacre of Jews in Russia," "Christians Openly Slay Israelites," and "Jewesses Outraged by Russians." The *New York Evening Journal* called the decree "an effort to fool the ignorant peasants into supporting an ignorant and brutal Tsar. . . . Good luck to the revolutionary, fighting Jews of Russia, trying to make a decent republican land of that oppressed soil."[30]

Some two sterile months after Nicholas had promised the Duma, liberals began to suspect that they had once again been tricked. They had a resolute leader now, for Paul Miliukov had returned from the United States. On May 8, he organized a Union of Unions, a broad liberal front that included the professional unions, moderate labor unions, and even a Social Revolutionary peasants union. He demanded that the government make good on its promise, and further that the Duma have legislative powers and be chosen by universal suffrage. America's response to Miliukov's demands was highly favorable. Already Miliukov had been cast as Founding Father, and now Americans felt that he was living up to the part. It was comforting to believe, as many did, that the professor had learned about republican institutions in America and carried the torch of freedom back to his own dark land. Here and there was disappointment over Miliukov's decision to call his movement a union—as well as a flurry of arguments, sometimes involving suffragettes, over the wisdom of his plan to give all citizens the right to vote.

Miliukov's demands were strengthened by news of events on the high seas. In a last desperate gamble for victory, Nicholas had ordered the forty ships of his Baltic Fleet to steam halfway around the world to Japan. Morale was low, the mood of some sailors revolutionary and of others fatalistic. American Bible salesmen, who boarded the vessels during a coaling stop at Port Said, reported sales of seven hundred volumes in less than two hours.[31] When the fleet reached the island of Tsushima, in the Sea of Japan, it was annihilated by Admiral Togo's battleships and torpedo boats.

Government impotence was further demonstrated a month later, on June 27, by an occurrence aboard the battleship *Potemkin,* cruising in the Black Sea off Odessa. Sailors had discovered worms in their meat and sought advice from the ship's doctor.

"The maggots are nothing but eggs which the flies have laid," the surgeon told them. "They are easily washed off with vinegar and water." Protests reached Captain Giliarovsky. In a conciliatory mood, he ordered that the meat be used to make bortsch, so that unwanted objects would not be noticed so easily.[32]

Still obstinate, the crew gathered on the main deck. "So it's mutiny, is it?" the captain called out. He described what it was like to swing from a yardarm, then offered one last chance: "Those who will eat their bortsch are dismissed. Anyone who remains can see for himself what we do to mutineers in the Navy."

One crewman, an SD named Afanasy Matushenko, had been waiting for a chance such as this. He killed Giliarovsky with a single shot, supervised the execution of other officers, and took over the *Potemkin* in the name of his party. Despite shortages of food and coal, as well as harassment by loyal naval forces, Matushenko kept the red flag flying for almost two weeks. At last he was forced to scuttle the vessel in Rumanian waters.

The battle of Tsushima and the *Potemkin* incident drew the attentions of the world to the inadequacies of the Russian Navy. The depletion of the navy interested Charles Schwab of Bethlehem Steel, who, hoping to close the biggest deal of his career, departed for St. Petersburg. Admirals in Washington told reporters of their contempt for Russian discipline. They were warned by the *Coast Seamen's Journal* to take heed of the *Potemkin* lesson and procure fresher meat for

American sailors. Some newspapers, even though they had been supporting the revolution, could not admire unpatriotic activities by men in the uniform of their country, it could set a bad example. In New York the *Times* said the mutineers ought to be hanged, and the *Herald* feared the spread of naval rebellion to all nations, wondering what would happen if anarchists collected a huge fleet of battleships and sent them out to prowl the civilized world. Yet the majority of recorded opinions showed approval of the mutiny even if it had ended in failure. It foreshadowed the day when all of Russia's armed forces would join the revolution.[33]

Miliukov, inferring the same, spoke often of the naval catastrophes in speeches he made urging the creation of a constitution. In an indirect manner, the battle of Tsushima had also helped the Tsar. It enabled him at long last to realize that the war was lost and that he needed a treaty with Japan at the earliest possible moment. Any Russian, no matter what his politics, could predict the harmful effects of peace upon the revolution. For the time being, at least, the empire's best regiments were far away in Manchuria, a condition that prompted Miliukov to accelerate his demands. He knew that he was working against time.

His pressure was strong enough to draw another round of promises from the Tsar. On August 19, Nicholas swore on an icon that arrangements for an election would be considered without delay. Although he said again that the Duma would have no power, the more moderate liberals decided to cooperate. They hoped that once the assembly was in operation, they could work to make it meaningful. Others, Miliukov among them, refused to compromise and vowed to continue the revolution until Russia had a real constitution.

Liberals made most of the Russian news during the summer of 1905. They appeared to be in control of the upheaval and to be shaping it to their ends.

Ironically, American affections cooled noticeably at a time when the revolution was showing its most attractive face.

Roosevelt

4. Roosevelt Rescues the Tsar

PRIOR TO 1905, Theodore Roosevelt's Russian policy had been similar to that of the American people. The president considered the Tsar to be ignorant, corrupt, brutal, barbaric, and immoral, and had said so in the presence of reporters. He approved wholeheartedly of the "average Russian" and would be delighted to see him "tread the path of orderly freedom, of civil liberty, and of a measure of self-government." He had played with the possibility of "going to extremes with Russia" after the pogrom of 1903. Early the next year, having perceived a Tsarist threat to American interests in the Far East, he had talked of war "if the Russians push us improperly and too evidently."[1]

During most of 1904, Roosevelt's moral preference for the revolution coincided with his appraisal of national interests. Since the Open Door note of 1900, the United States had been committed, at least on paper, to the protection of Chinese territories. Roosevelt viewed the Open Door policy as dangerously romantic. He knew that the nation's

Army of a few thousand men could not hope to fight a successful war on the Asian continent. Yet, to renege upon the guarantee would mean losing face, always a repugnant idea to one who prided himself on manliness. The Tsar's advance into Chinese Manchuria put Roosevelt on the spot, and he dreaded the day when he must decide whether or not to oppose Russia's armies.

That day never came. Roosevelt was jubilant when he heard of Japan's surprise attack upon the Russian fleet at Port Arthur. He was grateful to "a friend who was serving our purposes in the Orient," and raised glasses of champagne in the name of Japanese courage, honor, efficiency, and personal cleanliness. Those little yellow people, he said, were fighting like white men. In creating new heroes, the press needed no advice from the White House. Japan was pictured as remarkably similar to the United States—democratic, practical-minded, inventive, progressive, and not afraid of anything. She was especially admirable as an underdog, a tiny little people standing up to the world's largest nation. Americans who supported the Russian revolution automatically supported Japan. "It was Japan that fired the first effective gun for the liberation of the Russian people," the *Jewish Exponent* said. According to the *Springfield Republican*, "the Japanese are doing more to reform Russia than everything else in the world." They were fighting in the name of all free people, in the interests of civilization, said one writer. The Japanese, bent on territorial expansion, were quite possibly surprised to find themselves in so noble a role, but they learned how to play that role well. As the war continued they sent periodic warnings to the Tsar that he must grant his people civil and religious liberties or suffer the consequences. Japanese publicity releases described how captured Russian soldiers were begging to stay with their liberators, who gave them better treatment than they had received at home. Jewish prisoners were provided with rich foods, impressive housing, all the women they wanted, and elaborate Passover services. Some were made Knights of the Rising Sun. Thus Japan promoted her cause in the eyes of the world in general—and Jacob Schiff in particular. Schiff, a partner in the New York banking house of Kuhn, Loeb and Company, had been spending his own money to aid pogrom victims and the revolution. Early in the war, at a time when military experts were predicting Japan's ultimate defeat, he floated a twenty-five million dollar loan for the Tokyo government. By the war's end he had sponsored four more loans totaling two hundred million dollars, thus subsidizing half the war effort against Russia.[2]

Roosevelt kept an eye on the strategic picture. For a time he shouted "Bully!" after every Japanese victory. It was beginning to appear that the small nation could halt Russian expansion and maintain the Asian balance of power through her own efforts. If not, he might consider helping Japan. In July 1904, he asked the Navy Department to prepare plans for possible action at Vladivostok.[3]

Once again Japan relieved the president of decision-making burdens. In battle after battle, on the sea and in the siege trenches around Manchurian cities, she was proving that she was more than a match for Russia. Roosevelt began to hedge. He still hoped Japan would win "but not too overwhelmingly." Soon he was speaking of yellow peril as often as Slavic peril, and by the end of the year had become convinced that Japan was the greater menace to the balance of power. In the State Department, where enthusiasm for Japan had once been unrestrained, there were somber discussions of a Far Eastern Frankenstein which American policy had helped to create.[4]

In Roosevelt's altered formula for national interests, there was no place for the Russian revolution. He feared that if the Tsar's government collapsed, Japan could not be prevented from conquering all of Manchuria and perhaps the remainder of China. The president was also aware that a radical change in the structure of European alliances, where Russia was one of the balancing factors, could not possibly benefit the United States.

American diplomatic readjustments invariably have required moral readjustments. With his inherent fear of radicalism, Roosevelt had no trouble finding a number of fundamentally unwholesome qualities in the revolution. Even so, he could not bring himself to like the Russian government. He continued to believe that it represented all that was "most insincere, mendacious, and unscrupulous, and most reactionary." He could not think of the Tsar as anything but a "preposterous little creature" and was disgusted when someone told him that Nicholas "had acquired when a boy certain habits which were not discovered until they undoubtedly weakened him physically and morally." However repugnant Nicholas was to Roosevelt, Tsarism seemed to be the lesser of two evils. Roosevelt no longer ridiculed Russia's government when newspapermen were present. And he followed the advice of his ambassador in St. Petersburg, who had been pleading with him to stop writing "blunt, indiscreet, honest comments" about Nicholas, in view of the fact that Russian secret police were reading all of the president's letters before they were delivered to the embassy.[5]

Roosevelt undertook the task of improving Russian-American relations, which had gone from bad to worse over the past two years. Ambassador Cassini had begun to throw temper tantrums nearly every day, protesting United States diplomacy, the anti-Tsar press, or the prorevolutionary sentiment of the American people. His indignation was immense when he heard that a portrait of Nicholas had been mutilated at the St. Louis World's Fair. When the White House elevator broke down while he was on it, he accused the American government of plotting his death. Roosevelt told Secretary Hay to do all that he could to mollify the Russian, and, by May 1905, the World Today reported that "Count Cassini enjoys more cordial and intimate relations at the State Department than any other envoy of the present day."

Hay asked to be quoted on the fact that he regarded Cassini "most highly as a man, and that, moreover, his unquestionable ability as a diplomatist appeals . . . with particular force." On this point the Russian government did not agree. When it became clear that Cassini was sulking, unable to forgive his former tormentors, the Foreign Ministry called him home. His replacement was Baron R. R. Rosen, whose orders were "to change the tide of popular sentiment in favor of Russia."[6]

Roosevelt had undertaken this same task. Press opinion displeased him now that his policy ran counter to its main current. His *rapprochement* with Nicholas might be embarrassed, or even wrecked, by America's passion for the revolution; he was not sure how to solve the problem. As early as December of 1904 he had discussed the situation with Indiana Senator Albert Beveridge and German ambassador Speck von Sternberg, neither of whom could think of a solution. Bloody Sunday brought new distress. The president deplored what he thought to be the sensational, inflammatory, and irresponsible conduct of the press in reporting the event. Washington newsmen speculated that he was on the verge of doing or saying something that would "quiet public opinion."[7] But he was careful, as always, to protect his own prestige. This was hardly the time to speak kindly of Nicholas. He rode out the storm, maintaining a discreet silence while telegrams and letters, urging action against the Tsar, cluttered his mailroom.

Senators and representatives, similarly inundated, asked Roosevelt for guidance. He told them he would say absolutely nothing about the January affair in St. Petersburg, a statement that exasperated Congressman Robert Baker, Democrat from New York City. "The President does not voice the real sentiments of the people of the United States," he charged, threatening to sponsor a House resolution to that effect. He was informed by the Republican leadership that he would be expelled from Congress if he offered such a resolution.[8]

"Well, expel me," Baker erupted on the House floor. His speech dwelled at length upon the butchery of thousands of unarmed men, women, and children, one of the most dastardly crimes ever perpetrated, and asked that Congress, speaking for both the American government and people, officially condemn the Tsar as a murderer. Whatever the chances that his resolution would pass, Baker ruined them with oratorical grapeshot designed to finish off all his enemies. He denounced the president, the Republican party, conservative Democrats, the Supreme Court, and the cabinet. "Words fail me," he declared.

"It just as well that they do," Speaker Joseph Cannon interrupted. "The gentleman's time has expired." The resolution was easily defeated.

Revolutionary violence shared headlines with crushing Russian defeats at Port Arthur and Mukden. For Roosevelt these events were interrelated; Japanese victories were direct results of the revolution. Seeking greater "understanding of political and social conditions in Russia," he arranged to have an old friend, Cecil Spring-Rice, then attached to the British Embassy in St. Petersburg, brought to Washington for consultation. The president asked for the inside story—Was the revolution likely to succeed? Exactly how much was it hurting Russia's war effort? Would it be possible to end that war now, through friendly mediation, before the Tsar was weakened past all hope of recovery? Spring-Rice was sympathetic but allowed Roosevelt to know that, in view of his own country's alliance with Japan, he should not be expected to suggests ways and means for strengthening the government of Nicholas II.[9]

The president had decided to change his ambassador to Russia. He had come to view Robert S. McCormick, who had held the St. Petersburg post since 1902, as lazy and indecisive. McCormick had persisted in seeing the revolution as a complicated matter and was not even certain whether he was for it or against it. Wanting "a stronger hand," Roosevelt selected George von L. Meyer, one of the toughest bosses in the Republican party. Meyer took over the embassy in March 1905. His instructions were to make friends, gain the confidence of the Tsar and his advisors, and convince them that peace was an immediate necessity. "It will be hard work," Meyer wrote, "as the Russians are very much prejudiced against us." He wasted no time. At his first audience in the Winter Palace, moments after having presented his credentials, he plunged into a description of Roosevelt's plan for ending the war. Nicholas abruptly changed the subject due to the close proximity of the Tsarina Alexandra, his most warlike advisor. Several times in recent months she had created terrible scenes—crying, stamping her feet, and throwing croquet mallets—at the merest suggestion that her husband was considering negotiations with Japan. Meyer's *faux pas* did not prevent the Tsar from thinking him "charming . . . a fascinating talker and personality."[10]

Roosevelt no longer needed to ask British diplomats for information about the revolution. Meyer had orders to write daily reports on "the real meaning of the movement for so-called reforms" and send them directly to the White House rather than to the State Department. Unlike McCormick, the new ambassador was decisive. He had definite views on the revolution, and the knack for expressing them without wasting time. Basically, he felt that the revolution was socialistic, led by men whose motives were unpatriotic, absurd, and unreasonable. "I find that the number of working hours per year is much less than the number of working hours per year in the U.S." he wrote to Roosevelt. He viewed the revolution as distasteful, horrible, an imminent peril, and a real danger to the efforts of good men who sought peace on earth; and he spoke of his great relief upon hearing of revolutionary defeats, the "joyful news of a partial return to normal conditions."[11]

The battle of Tsushima startled the ambassador. He wrote bitterly that both liberals and radicals were celebrating the defeat of their own country. Sensing that Tsushima threatened to renew revolutionary confidence and to inspire cataclysms that might destroy the Tsarist system, he told Roosevelt that a peace treaty was imperative.[12]

Germany's Wilhelm II was equally insistent that peace be achieved. Fearing Japan's great victory would lead to grave disorders and even to attempts upon the Tsar's life, he urged Roosevelt not to delay his peacemaking efforts.[13]

The president had certainly been striving for peace, as evidenced by his repeated instructions to Meyer, his White House talks with Russian and Japanese representatives, and dozens of letters in which he sought the cooperation of non-belligerent powers. These had been wary moves, subdued by anxiety that Japan would resent a blatant effort to stop her string of triumphs. When Roosevelt learned that Japan also wished to negotiate (she was running short of men and money), he was free to proceed openly. It was now quite likely, he believed, that a peacemaker would win the gratitude and admiration of almost all the world. On June 10, he issued formal invitations to a peace conference at Portsmouth, New Hampshire.

Convinced by Tsushima that the war was hopeless, Nicholas responded gratefully to the offer, but he was beset by delays. The Tsarina and certain ministers were doing all they could to stall arrangements for the conference. Some advisors were simply stubborn, too proud to admit defeat; and others preferred to wait until the Russian army had won a battle, thus creating a better bargaining position. Lethargy in the Foreign Ministry stemmed from resentment of Roosevelt for having bypassed that office in sending his invitation directly to the Tsar. All this bickering appalled the president. "Oh Lord, I have been growing nearly mad in the effort to get Russia and Japan together," he exclaimed. Cables received from Meyer in June and early July were not reassuring. Russian armies were in retreat, and there were rumors that Japan was no longer in the mood to negotiate, at least not until she had overrun all of Manchuria as well as the Vladivostok area of Russian Siberia. The Tsar's government was crumbling, Meyer said, pointing out that the need for peace was urgent so that the army could be transferred from the Manchurian front to the streets of Russian cities. "I have believed heretofore that revolution is . . . improbable, but events of the past week have altered conditions. . . . The disturbances at Lodz, the Marines revolting in Libau, the successful [Potemkin] mutiny show progress made by revolutionists. . . . Strikes are on the increase, and internal affairs go from bad to worse. . . . It is impossible to close one's eyes to the peril which hangs over Russia."[14]

Presidential cables arrived in London, Paris, Vienna, and Berlin at the rate of two or three a week, all pleading for help in ending Russian procrastination. Cables to St. Petersburg were addressed to Meyer, but Roosevelt asked that he show them to Nicholas. These analyzed political conditions in Russia and spelled out the reasons that nation "for her own good must make peace . . . at all hazards and all cost" so that Nicholas could "turn his attention to internal affairs." The ambassador, cablegrams in hand, was kept on the run to the palace. When the Foreign Ministry refused to grant audiences, Meyer threatened to burst unannounced into the throne room. By one means or another he delivered all of Roosevelt's advice. When the Tsar at last named delegates (Sergei Witte and Ambassador R. R. Rosen) to the peace conference, Meyer wrote to his chief, "I have a strong feeling that your note was instrumental in assisting to bring this about."[15]

Representatives of Russia and Japan, meeting at Portsmouth, New Hampshire, argued throughout most of August. Their anxious host wanted to "knock their heads together," for often it appeared that the conference to which he had attached his personal prestige would end in failure. Japan had won the war, and Roosevelt did not oppose her absorption of Korea and Russia's leaseholds in South Manchuria. But Japan wanted more—all of the Island of Sakhalin and a large cash indemnity. Russia would not agree to an indemnity, claiming that to pay it would drain the Tsar's treasury at a time when money was desperately needed. It was this issue that presented the peacemaker with his greatest challenge.

An amateur Machiavelli, Roosevelt preferred to work behind the scenes, inviting individual Russians and Japanese to sessions on his yacht and in his house at Oyster Bay. He cajoled and blustered, bluffed and double-bluffed, hoping one side or the other would give in. Attempting inscrutability, he gave each side the definite impression that he would support it in the end, thereby inspiring each to hold out for as long as possible. Ultimately he backed the Russian position. The importance of his role has been a matter of much historical debate: Was the Tsar allowed to remain solvent mainly because of Roosevelt's manipulations, or was the diplomatic finesse of Sergei Witte, Russia's chief delegate, the more decisive factor? In any case, Roosevelt's name was powerfully associated with a treaty that gave Japan neither money nor Sakhalin's upper half, a treaty viewed throughout the world as an astonishing victory for the Tsar.

With his usual disdain for false modesty, the president delighted in the congratulations pouring in from other countries. "Your personal energetic efforts . . . brought the peace," Nicholas cabled. "My country will gratefully recognize the great part you have played." The German Kaiser too was relieved. "The whole of mankind must unite and will do so in thanking you for the great boon you have given it," Wilhelm told Roosevelt, and he said almost the same thing in a note to the Tsar, "Roosevelt . . . has really done a great work for your country." In his cabled congratulations from St. Petersburg Spring-Rice said, "To all of us here . . . the peace is directly and solely due to the President's personal intervention." The widespread acceptance of this view was indicated a few months later when Roosevelt was awarded the Nobel Peace Prize. Japan's thank-you notes were polite but reserved. Its government was relieved that the exhausting war was over, but also felt that glorious victories should have brought greater profits than those received at Portsmouth. Tokyo newspapers expressed the feeling more aggressively, calling Roosevelt a white devil, wicked, Japan's worst enemy. Crowds rampaged through the streets of Tokyo, spitting at Americans, striking them with sticks, and throwing stones and rotten fruit at the United States consulate. Japanese sentiment foreshadowed future troubles, but for the moment all was well with the president. He prided himself on having maintained the balance of power, and found auxiliary satisfaction in having stopped a bloody war in the name of civilization. Warmed by praise from the four corners of the earth, he began to say that he had acted "on an exclusively altruistic basis."[16]

A few disagreed. There were Russians who believed that Roosevelt's humanitarianism left much to be desired. They called his Nobel Prize a tragic irony. Relating the treaty solely to their revolutionary interests, they accused the president of having worked consciously and diligently against them. The cavalry hero of San Juan Hill had ridden again at Portsmouth, said revolutionaries, rescuing the Tsar at the last moment. Miliukov's liberals were especially bitter, for they believed their government had been on the verge of bowing to demands for a meaningful constitution.[17]

The *New York World* said that Roosevelt must be held responsible for all oppression to be endured by the Russian people in the future. "The people of Russia will lose by the Treaty of Portsmouth," the *Hartford Daily Courant* said, and continued: "It is called a triumph for Russia. Which Russia? For the autocracy—not the people. President Roosevelt has done better for the Russian government than it deserved." An old friend of the president's, John Burroughs, disappointedly said, "I believe it would have been better to pay the

price of a more protracted war in order to have a general
house cleaning in Russia." An old enemy, socialist Daniel
DeLeon, reacted in a manner that surprised no one: "Peace
was dictated . . . by Roosevelt, who acted as the representative of the world's labor oppressors." Mark Twain described
Portsmouth as "the greatest calamity that has ever befallen
civilization. The Russians were within an inch of civil
liberty, but it has been snatched from them. . . . No war was
ever charged with a higher mission. . . . That mission is now
defeated and Russia's chains re-riveted. . . . I think the Tsar
will now withdraw the small humanities that have been
forced from him, and resume his medieval barbarisms with
a relieved spirit and an immeasurable joy. . . . One more
battle would have abolished the waiting chains of millions of
unborn Russians, and I wish it could have been fought."[18]

Roosevelt was aware of Portsmouth's consequences. While
he probably regretted the worst of these, they simply were
not so important to him as America's interest in preserving
power balances on two continents. He thought of himself as
a realist. Yet this manner of justification was not quite
enough for an American, a progressive, and a man who
wanted to be morally right as well as realistic. Hence his
after-the-fact interest in the humanitarian aspects of peace,
and his growing tendency to think of the Russian revolution
as an essentially sinister movement. In letters to Meyer he
most heartily agreed that the revolution was socialistic and
that the cause of democracy had been hopeless from the
start in a nation of lazy, illiterate, and backward people.

"I find some disappointment among our people over the
terms of the peace made at Portsmouth," said Elihu Root,
Secretary of State since the death of John Hay in July. While
disappointment certainly was evident in the remarks of Mark
Twain and others, it was surprisingly limited considering
the extent of prorevolutionary sentiment only a few months
before. In February the president had been extremely careful

not to publicize his efforts to help the Tsar. In August he spoke openly of this policy, due in part to what he called "a perceptible swinging around" of public opinion. Like Roosevelt, many Americans had grown fearful of Japan, especially after the shock of Tsushima. Senator Beveridge detected another reason for pro-Tsar sentiments—disenchantment with the revolution itself, either through boredom or suspicion, or perhaps both. "I think that American public opinion is gradually veering around to the right view on these matters, just as it always does if given time," the senator from Indiana said.[19]

One plan to bring support to the Tsar was a public relations campaign conducted by antirevolutionary visitors to the United States. The Russian government had assigned a double mission to Ambassador Rosen and Sergei Witte. Besides negotiating peace with Japan, they were supposed "to try to change American sympathies in regard to Russia."[20]

The day after moving into the embassy, Baron Rosen embarked upon a full schedule of press conferences and speaking engagements. He praised all things American, just as Paul Miliukov had done earlier for other purposes. He stressed the traditional friendship between the two nations, never failing to mention that the United States, during its own rebellion in 1861, had received diplomatic support from Russia. The character of the Tsar had been distorted by his enemies, said Rosen, for here in truth was a deeply religious man, one who loved America, played games on the lawn with his wife and children, and wept frequently over the plight of his people. Rosen was charming, the *Financial Review* said, "far more appealing in manner than last winter's tawdry assortment of travellers from Russia." Meanwhile the ambassador's wife was entertaining at a pace considered quite unusual for the summer season. A society commentator reported that Baroness Rosen was likely to become "a leading factor in the social life at Washington, where she [was] already well known and much liked."[21]

As minister of finance Sergei Witte had outmaneuvered the United States (which he detested) in tariff competition, had obtained advantageous interest rates on loans from France, and had found means of subsidizing the development of Russian capitalism, including a railway to Vladivostok. Colleagues in other ministries considered Witte to be a subtle intriguer, a stockbroker's son who had connived to climb to a position of power and there rub shoulders with aristocrats. Although he talked incessantly of his political conservatism and his dedication to the preservation of Tsarist autocracy, he had opposed the bloody policies of Plehve and Trepov, as well as the war with Japan, on the basis that such policies were self-destructive, bringing revolution ever closer. He had advised Nicholas to grant reforms similar to those of the eighteenth-century benevolent despots, urging that such reforms would in the long run strengthen rather than weaken the autocracy. Kellogg Durland, one of the University Settlement travelers, called Witte more a stratagem than a man and believed that his subtle maneuvers could injure the revolution far more effectively than could Trepov's Cossacks.[22]

Witte enjoyed diplomacy, especially when it became the game of flattery and bluff that he played so well at Portsmouth. His other American mission, public relations, was repugnant to one who so admired aristocracy. Yet he admitted its necessity and knew that he was clever enough to succeed in this task too. He developed a "deliberate plan" to win friends in the United States. He decided, "in view of the tremendous influence of the press in America, to show it every attention and to be accessible to all its representatives." To all Americans he would "behave with democratic simplicity and without a shadow of snobbishness . . . thank everyone and talk with all kinds of people . . . and treat everybody, of whatever social position, as an equal." Witte later revealed that "this behavior was a heavy strain . . . as all acting is to be unaccustomed, but it surely was worth the trouble. . . . My personal behavior may . . . account for the transformation of American public opinion."[23]

For lectures Witte chose such topics as American greatness, the traditional warmth of Russian-American relations, and the innate decency of the Tsar. Reporters were fascinated, writing of his flashing smile, the rakish tilt of his hat, and firm, businessman's handshake. It became Witte's habit to drape an arm across a journalist's shoulders, to ask about the wife and children, or to tell a joke about the traveling salesman and the peasant's daughter from a little place outside Smolensk. (His British advisor, E. J. Dillon, had helped him prepare a repertoire of such jokes and stories.) He exhibited a keen interest in baseball, once handing his walking stick to a reporter and asking to be shown the proper way to hold a bat. He carried red and black jawbreakers in paper sacks with which to delight the youngsters. On the Boston-to-Portsmouth train he traversed every coach, shaking hands with all passengers, and at his destination hugged the engineer and kissed the conductor while photographical powders exploded. Witte's artful chatter failed to impress Roosevelt, who described the envoy as utterly cynical, untruthful, and unscrupulous. The president regretted that his support of Russia would promote the career of a man he thoroughly disliked.[24]

Witte's public success resulted in part from the excellent advice of E. J. Dillon. As a free-lance correspondent in St. Petersburg, he had pleased Witte with his attitude toward the revolution. Dillon's Russia, presented in articles sent to America, was full of balalaikas, waltzing noblewomen, graceful troikas, red and gold guardsmen snapping to attention, and other bright trappings which had once made St. Petersburg one of the gayest and prettiest cities in Europe. Lamentably, the revolution threatened to sweep away all of these assets. Witte asked Dillon to accompany him to America as a confidant and special advisor. In addition to providing the diplomat with pointers on popularity, Dillon himself was a valuable publicist, providing newspapers and magazines with his own fresh versions of Russia's inside story. Revolution, he revealed, was the great enemy of the reform movement; gradualism was the American way, and it must be the Russian way as well. At this very hour, without doubt, he told American readers, important reforms were being considered by the wise and liberal men in the Tsar's government. Loyal to his benefactor, Dillon said that the qualities of the Russian leaders were best represented by Sergei Witte himself— persevering, hardworking, sincere, trustworthy, a doer rather than a thinker, and a self-made man of business. "Witte is to his countrymen what Anglo-Saxon America is to the rest of the world,"[25] Dillon said in an article for the *Review of Reviews*.

Public response more than fulfilled the press agent's hopes. Witte's doings made front-page news even in Alabama and Texas, and his life story was the subject of numerous magazine articles. His flashing smile and rakish headgear adorned Sunday rotogravures. Journalists often surpassed Dillon in their praise of a man who was "very American, for a Russian." They described the latest celebrity as a genuine progressive businessman, with a judicious sense of conservatism, a man who would make capitalism a going concern in Russia. It was confidently written that Witte would be named prime minister (though he would make a better president, some said), when he returned home. If so, newsmen said, the internal development of Russia would astonish the world. Excusing his opposition to the revolution, journalists credited him with possessing a heart as well as a brain, along with a great and simple soul—the Russian people could only hope to prosper from his liberality, providing they saw the wisdom of disowning the radicals among them. Readers of the *New York Tribune* were introduced to the Abraham Lincoln of Russia, a man of humble birth who by acts of Christian charity would remove the chains from the people. Inferring much from reports of Witte's nonaristocratic origins, some writers reached the conclusion that he had been a peasant lad, born in a hut on the steppes, and had split ties with an ax while building railroads across Siberia.[26]

Witte's popularity was transferable only to a degree. He could not overnight capture American affections for his sovereign and state. Yet the old bitterness was disappearing. Editors were trying, as the *Newark Daily Advertiser* put it, "to understand a system too often maligned, even if it is an autocracy."[27]

Thus there was some truth in Witte's ebullient report on his mission: "When I left the transatlantic republic, practically the whole press was our champion. The press, in its turn, was instrumental in bringing about a complete change in the public opinion of the country—in favor of my person and of the cause I upheld."[28] Nicholas must have been impressed. A few days after his return, Witte was named prime minister and given something he wanted even more—admission to the nobility as a count.

Breshkovsky

5. Countermarch

AMONG SEVERAL ASPECTS of American response to the revolution—diplomatic issues, travelers in Russia, treatment of Russian visitors to the United States, and questions of financial aid to revolutionaries or to the Tsar—the matter of press opinion must also be included.

In the summer of 1905, President Roosevelt, Senator Beveridge, Sergei Witte, and others said that public opinion was undergoing a change in the Tsar's favor. While it is probably true that these spokesmen were correct in their appraisal of "public opinion," the present study confines itself only to opinions stated editorially in selected organs of the press. Within this area, certainly, views on Russia shifted dramatically. Out of fifty-six important general-circulation magazines and newspapers, forty-nine definitely had favored the revolution in January 1905. By December of the same year, forty-two of the forty-nine could be counted as supporters of the Tsar's regime. Those editors who bothered to explain their change of mind cited their reason as increased fear of Japan, a desire not to oppose President Roosevelt's policies, and above all the "discovery" that socialism rather than democracy was the goal of Russian revolutionaries. The same change of opinion (largely for the same reasons) is reflected in selected business, farm, labor, Catholic, and Protestant publications, but American socialists demonstrated increasing sympathy toward the revolution during 1905. Reactions remained mixed in the Jewish press.

The nonradical Jewish press was represented primarily by the *American Israelite*, published in Cincinnati; *Jewish Exponent*, Philadelphia; *Jewish Independent*, Cleveland; *American Hebrew*, New York; *Jewish Comment*, Baltimore; and *Menorah*, the official organ of the Jewish Chautauqua Society, based in Philadelphia. All circulated nationally, were owned by Jews of German extraction, and showed little sympathy toward the current greenhorn immigration from Russia. While such papers could not have been expected to alter anti-Tsarist views, they grew increasingly insistent during 1905 that these views were based upon something other than love of revolution.

For years American Jews had read lurid accounts of fire, sword, and drunken mobs, of heavy casualties, and of the Russian government's connivance in pogroms. "God help us never to become too accustomed to these stories," the *American Israelite* said, "and never to experience anything but shock and rage while reading them."[1]

Some Jews felt that to support the revolution was to work in behalf of the peasant, that detestable creature whose bigotry became operational at a word from his priest or by a cup of government vodka. The *American Israelite* wanted nothing to do with the Russian people, viewed as idolatrous, inhumane, barbaric, bigoted, and superstitious. It saw revolution as attractive only as a plague on both the Winter Palace and peasant huts. All Russians must be "purged with fire and blood until they are fit to humbly take their place . . . at the foot of civilized nations," said the *Israelite*.[2]

Russian Jews of New York's East Side, firmly dedicated to revolution, could not allow hatred for peasants to harm the larger purpose. Peasants, they held, were merely ignorant tools of the government's pogrom policy. Finding resolutions for all paradoxes, *Bundists* and sds painted signs, cranked mimeograph machines, and organized mass meetings and parades. Most influential among New York's fourteen Yiddish newspapers was Abraham Cahan's *Daily Forward.* Cahan's view was typically uncomplicated: "My heart is jumping for joy and inspiration. We have a revolution in Russia! A real People's Revolution! A Proletarian Worker's Revolution!" Using public opinion polls, characterized more by enthusiasm than scientific method, Cahan proved that all American Jews were ardent supporters of the revolution. Somehow, during busy 1905, he found time to write a novel, *The White Terror and the Reds,* about a Russian nobleman who fell in love with a magnificently buxom Jewess, turned socialist for her, went to prison, and was rescued in the end by Social Democrats. The book received hostile reviews in the German Jewish press.[3]

Wealthier, better-established Jews were embarrassed by the East Siders, with their radical politics and imprudent conduct. The presence of these greenhorns was in fact a threat. A heightened anti-Semitism, due in large measure to the immigration of hundreds of thousands of refugees from Russia, was everywhere evident. The *New York Herald* gave doomsday reports: "The engulfing tide of immigrants continued yesterday when 12,678 arrived on nine ships. At least eighty percent were Hebrews." Patriotic societies complained that the country was filling up with undesirables, that the national character was becoming blurred, and that Anglo-Saxon blood was being contaminated. It was feared that New York would become a new Jerusalem, with Jews steadily gaining political power and taking over Wall Street. The *New York Sun* was horrified to learn that Jews had obtained more than half of the teachers' licenses issued by the city in August 1905. New York's district attorney said that it was no longer possible to get convictions in cases of crimes committed against Jews. Pressure mounted for new laws restricting immigration, and native-born Jews often agreed that something must be done. "How to control this tide of immigration is one of the great problems of the age," Simon Wolf, president of B'nai B'rith, told a 1905 convention of that organization.[4]

The conservative papers emphasized that most of their readers did not want to be associated with the newcomers. It was said that demonstrators and propagandists were not real Jews, that they were socialists; and socialism could not be harmonized with Jewish principles. New York's Yiddish papers were called worse specimens of yellow journalism than even the products of Hearst and Pulitzer. Yet no Jewish paper could ignore the pogroms. The conservative publications acknowledged that here was a problem of deep concern, but one that could only be solved gradually and in the fullness of time. Someday the right would conquer, the conservatives said, and the voice of God would be heard. According to the *Israelite*, the tactics of radical East Siders, like those of their comrades in Russia, could result only in irritating the Tsar and causing greater slaughters.[5]

By the summer of 1905 the *Israelite* was advocating a nonviolent plan for stopping pogroms. "Pressure may be brought to bear by the Jewish capitalists of more favored lands," it suggested. "Let every Jewish financier the world over decline to subscribe for Russian bonds . . . until reforms are made." Jacob Schiff, floater of the Japanese loans, had already written to the Rothschilds, Mendelssohns, and other European banking houses, hoping to convince them to say no to the Tsar. The London branch of Rothschilds agreed with Schiff, but elsewhere results were disappointing, leading some of Schiff's discouraged friends to say that bankers could not be swayed by sentiment and that Jewish rights could not be bought. "Maybe not," the *Israelite* said, "but it is worth a try." The time for such efforts was now, Schiff urged, due to the presence in New York of one Sergei Witte, who, for a Tsarist official, appeared to be quite gracious and agreeable.[6]

As part of his public relations campaign, Witte had planned "that in view of the considerable influence of the Jews on the press and on other aspects of American life, especially in New York, not to exhibit any hostility toward them." Therefore, on a steaming day in mid-August, East Side refugees found a different sort of Russian in their midst, one impeccably tailored in summer grays from bowler to spats, who treated children to ice cream and spoke often of the Little Father's affection for his non-Christian subjects.[7]

Witte also agreed to confer with a delegation of Jewish bankers, businessmen, and editors. Here was undeniable proof of his liberal, democratic, and progressive attitudes, *Review of Reviews* said. The meeting began peacefully enough, due to the meliorative talents of Simon Wolf and Adolf Kraus, both representing B'nai B'rith. They respectfully submitted that the Russian government should re-examine its policy concerning pogroms and do what it could to extend civil rights to Jews. Witte's answer was characteristically good-humored. He certainly agreed in principle, he said, yet there were practical questions that he raised—Were Jews ready for civil liberties, considering their political and religious attitudes? Would not the granting of such rights enrage other Russians and thus do Hebrews more harm than good?[8]

Listening to Witte, Jacob Schiff could not restrain his anger. He had invested too much time and money in the cause to allow it to be dismissed in tones so blandly condescending. Wolf lost his temper too, shouting that the Tsar must reckon with American Jews. New York merchant Oscar Straus tried to calm his friends. He thought it highly unlikely that Witte could be moved by emotional displays of any kind. Only money could influence him, Straus said. The Tsar's government was eternally in need of foreign loans, and that need had never been greater than at present. As *Menorah* reported later, the bankers "delivered an ultimatum." There would be no loans to Russia until her Jews were given full civil and religious liberties.[9]

Witte appeared to be unconcerned. Money seemed to interest him no more than supplications and threats. Yet the subject had intrigued him only a few days earlier, during a Hudson River cruise aboard J. P. Morgan's yacht. Morgan had promised to manage the Russian loan himself. He insisted, Witte said later, "that I should not enter into any negotiations with the Jewish group of bankers headed by Jacob Schiff. I relied upon his promise of assistance."[10] Expressing relief at having eluded the grasp of Hebrew moneylenders, Witte did not know that he had met a better fox than himself. This he would learn when Morgan revealed his terms.

Now it was the turn of radical Jews to jeer and to say they wanted nothing to do with conservatives. Newspapers differed in reporting details of Witte's meeting with the bankers, but one thing was clear—the Jewish establishment had gone hat-in-hand to a Tsarist official. East Side papers called the meeting degrading and humiliating. When one of its participants, Adolf Kraus, tried to speak in a Chicago synogogue, he was chanted down with insults, and several people were injured in a riot that followed. Russia's Jewish press joined the uproar. The bankers were contemptible, the *Vilna Hasunan* said. St. Petersburg's *Der Fraind* commented: "Ho! not from the hands of capitalists shall help come to the Jews of Russia. . . . People who have fought for their rights . . . cannot condone cringing. We do not beg, and forbid others to do so in our name."[11]

Divisions among American Jews were never deeper than in September 1905, on the eve of Russia's bloodiest pogrom.

Roman Catholic weeklies applauded the revolution in its early stages. Attention centered on Poland, considered the most important example of suppressed religious liberties. This special interest ended with the Tsar's Easter ukase of 1905, which granted religious freedom to all minorities except Jews. Papers such as the *Catholic Mirror*, of the Baltimore archdiocese; *Catholic News*, New York; and *Catholic World*, a national monthly published in New York by the Paulist Fathers, began to question the value of the revolution and America's interest in it. They felt that there should be similar concern for priests and nuns whose properties currently were being confiscated by the French government, and that British tyranny in Ireland was more savage than anything witnessed in Russia. The *Catholic Standard and Times*, of the Philadelphia archdiocese, opposed the revolution on grounds that so many Jews were for it. Pogroms, it asserted, were the only logical way to deal with those "universally hated people who threatened to ruin all nations." One had only to look at America, now being inundated by "the world's most prolific race . . . more responsible for the high crime rate than hard-working Italian immigrants, and . . . much louder and more profane" than Catholic newcomers in general. Except for the *Standard and Times*, major Catholic papers condemned pogroms and continued to do so even after they became convinced that the revolution was a dangerous socialistic movement.[12]

To Protestant spokesmen, the revolution was symbolic of fundamental moral truths and consequently was deserving of either total support or total rejection. Christian soldiers marched, wheeled, and came marching back in the opposite direction. During 1905 the national *Presbyterian* applied identical terms—pious goal, Godly mission, and glorious crusade—first to the revolution and then to the Tsarist cause. Likewise the Baptist *Watchman*, of Boston, stoked the fires of Hell for Nicholas in February and for his opponents in November. Denominational papers gave several reasons for changing sides. The *Presbyterian* had come to admire "the piety, purity, and high social standing" of the royal family. The *Christian Evangelist,* a St. Louis publication of the Christian Church, could no longer tolerate "the notorious dissipation and drunkenness of the average Russian," who must "repent and cleanse himself—then, and only then, will he prove himself worthy of democracy's blessings." The national *Lutheran Witness* had detested the Tsar for his cruel treatment of five million Lutherans in Russia's Baltic and Finnish provinces. Upon learning of the Easter ukase, the *Witness* suggested that all pastors offer prayers of thanksgiving to a wise and beneficent monarch. Since the ukase apparently would allow Russia's twenty-five thousand Baptists to worship as they pleased, the *Watchman* and *Christian Index,* of Atlanta, were enabled to turn with free conscience against the revolution.[13]

Fear of radicalism was the overriding reason most Catholics and Protestants changed their minds. By late summer the *Watchman* was detecting telltale signs of Red activities in Russia. The Methodist *Christian Advocate,* of Nashville, begged God's forgiveness: "If we had known last winter that the uprising was whipped up by red anarchists, we never would have befriended it." The *Presbyterian* described assorted horrors of anarchy, and the *Christian Observer,* a Louisville paper of the same denomination, probed socialism for its true meaning: "The fact remains for us, who believe in God, that riches and poverty do not come to us by chance but by His Fatherly Will. God makes rich and He keeps poor. Socialism, in seeking to alter this, strikes at the very basis of religion." The *Catholic Standard and Times* reminded readers that it had been one of the few papers staunchly opposed to the revolution from the very beginning. "The conduct of the American press," it said, "has been infamously one-sided. . . . The savage hatred of the Russian government shown by these rabid organs is utterly unaccountable, unless on the hypothesis that Hebrew influence prevails in their management. . . . Now, at last, they are realizing the truth, that the revolution has been entirely the work of Nihilists and Socialists."[14]

In the beginning, many American businessmen appeared to be firm friends of revolution in Russia. Their organizing abilities and interest in group activities were chiefly responsible for the popular, if not the financial, success of the fundraising tours in early 1905. Men of commerce and industry dominated the Friends of Russian Freedom, as well as myriad local committees set up to entertain freedom fighters, and the Miliukovs and Breshkovskys alike were warmly applauded when they spoke to noontime luncheon clubs. Business journals saw the revolution as a middle-class struggle against despotism. Zemstvos were said to resemble American Chambers of Commerce. The *Chicago Tribune* asserted that Russian liberals were fighting for free enterprise, seeking to end government restrictions that hindered industrial growth.[15]

A few financiers, however, had invested money in the Tsar. At the time of Bloody Sunday, two insurance companies, New York Life and The Equitable, held twenty-seven million dollars in Russian government bonds. It made no difference to Wall Street, the *New York Times* said, whether Russia was an autocracy or a republic or a socialist state, just so long as she remained solvent. It stood to reason that if the wrong sort of people took over, the Tsar's debts might be repudiated. The American investment was actually small compared with that of British and German bankers, and especially the French who had nearly two billion dollars in Russian holdings. Even so, Frank Vanderlip of New York's National City Bank foresaw grave consequences should the revolution continue to gain ground. Panics in London and Paris markets would result in foreigners selling off their American securities. *Bradstreet's,* the *Commercial and Financial Chronicle,* and the *American Banker,* all published in

New York, wholeheartedly agreed with Vanderlip. "Stability must be maintained"; "The Tsar is stupid to allow the demonstrations to go as far as they do"; "This rebellion must be stopped"; these papers said.[16]

Jewish Comment accused President Roosevelt of buckling under to financial interests. His frantic efforts to end the Russo-Japanese War were alleged to involve pressure from bankers. Hearst's *New York Evening Journal* issued a "Warning to Bankers! . . . Don't invest in any Russian securities whatsoever. You are simply betting on the Tsar's continued power when you make such an investment."[17]

The warning was ignored. Investments in Russia increased slowly during the summer of 1905, then rose sharply after the Portsmouth Conference. Sergei Witte, it seemed, had found a way to thank the United States "for the great gift of peace." At a farewell meeting with Roosevelt, he announced a long list of tariff reductions on American products. He emphasized the unilateral nature of these cuts, saying that Russia expected no reciprocal gestures in return. Businessmen became Witte's greatest admirers, not only because of his rags-to-riches story, but also for the marvelous trading opportunities he was offering them. With the war over, his country would need all manner of industrial and consumer goods. *Dun's Review* carried provocative articles on the money that could be made in Russia "as soon as the existing internal difficulties [were] adjusted." Witte scoffed at these difficulties. He assured everyone that the revolution was over. Moreover, he promised, the Tsar would deal quickly and efficiently with any remaining malcontents.[18]

With his firm handshake and way of looking a man straight in the eye, Witte could not be doubted. Entrepreneurs made sailing arrangements, and accounts of farewell parties appeared in New York's society pages in late September and early October. A hundred friends toasted George Perkins and J. P. Morgan, Jr., off for St. Petersburg to complete negotiations on the loan recently discussed by

Witte and Morgan, Sr. Also departing were John Wanamaker, Thomas Fortune Ryan, Thomas Purdy, Charles R. Flint, R. T. Grass, Frederick Corse, and W. E. Smith. Some were bond buyers. Some wanted to build factories and bridges, set up Russian branches of American corporations, or expand facilities already in operation. A representative of James J. Hill carried plans for a New York-to-St. Petersburg railroad, the construction of which was to begin immediately after the problem of the Bering Straits was worked out. Lesser salesmen had cases full of samples and brochures on plumbing fixtures, shoes, typewriters, nails, cosmetics, health tonics, bicycles, small firearms, roller skates, and pianos. Smith & Wesson's agent was turned back at customs.[19]

To those allowed to enter St. Petersburg, discouragement came with the realization that Sergei Witte's statements on Russian tranquillity had been grossly exaggerated.

Labor publications, while approving the outbreak of revolution, were more restrained than the general press. Only Bloody Sunday provoked interest that was in any way unique —pride in the Putilov workers for having been well behaved and modest in their demands, with never a hint of radicalism; nonetheless they had been shot down like dogs. "Never has an event so forcibly demonstrated the righteousness of labor's cause," said the *United Mine Workers' Journal,* a weekly published in Indianapolis.[20]

The unions, with so many problems of their own, had little time for sentiment that could not be attached to practical goals. Analogy proved irresistible. A labor journalist, setting out to describe working conditions at Putilov or in Siberian mines, invariably found himself in Pittsburgh or West Virginia before his article was half finished. A transition sentence in *Elevator Constructor,* a Chicago monthly, is typical: "Thus it can be seen that horrible conditions exist in the domain of the Tsar, but how can these compare with Pennsylvania serfdom, where thousands of persons, many of them boys under the age of twelve, suffocated last year in the mines, or died by the bullets of a militia more brutalized than any Cossack regiment." The *New York Evening Journal* considered such stories detrimental to the interests of the Russian people: "American workers are gaining the impression that they are worse off than Russians, and this will have harmful effects upon their contributions to fund drives for the revolution."[21]

Labor was obsessed by fear of immigration. By late summer of 1905 a number of publications, such as *Blacksmith's Journal*, Chicago; *Meatcutter's Journal*, Philadelphia; *Lather*, Cleveland; the national *Knights of Labor Journal;* and others, were in open opposition to the revolution on grounds that it was creating hardships by forcing undesirable people to swarm to America, where they were willing to work for five cents a day. *Elevator Constructor* held that Russian Jews were "cheap artisans of every known trade . . . racially incompatible . . . next to the Japanese the most backboneless people in the world and . . . always willing to be scabs." Many labor editors encouraged the Tsar to crush the revolution as quickly as possible. Like business editors, they spoke of Russia's need to establish order and maintain stable conditions.[22]

Labor unions were extremely sensitive to the fact that many Americans associated union organizations with radicalism. Always trying to illustrate conservative feelings, union spokesmen lectured Russian workers on the proper means of achieving ends. "It is not desirable to meet force with force," San Francisco's *Coast Seamen's Journal* advised. "Respect for property is the first law," the *Lather* said. The *Knights of Labor Journal* was deeply concerned that Russian workers were turning socialist due to the fact that "being without culture and education, they lack intelligence. . . . Experience has shown that ownership of the land by the communities has discouraged the industrious by making them pay for the idler as well as for themselves." The *United*

Mine Workers' Journal had "no wish to appear snobbish," but if Russian workmen really wanted to improve themselves "they must be more cultured, more educated, and more respectful of law and order, which are the traits which mark the trades union movement in America."[23]

That most influential of labor leaders, Samuel Gompers, spoke with great care. He could not ignore Russia, for as president of the American Federation of Labor (AFL) he was often pressed to contribute statements, speeches, and union funds to the fight against tyranny. Following Bloody Sunday he wrote a letter to Father Gapon (undelivered), and later wrote to Witte and conversed with Baron Rosen at a garden party in Washington. In each case, he revealed in *American Federationist*, he had called for liberty, justice, and democracy in Russia. Yet he was increasingly aware that the revolution was "smirched by atrocities and crime," and he feared that Russian workers were "really socialists." Saying that he was ill or too busy, he declined invitations even to anti-pogrom dinners and meetings. He turned down the Friends of Russian Freedom with the excuse that their printed invitation did not bear the union label.[24]

At its 1905 convention, the AFL passed a number of anti-immigrant and antisocialist resolutions. E. L. Jordan of the Copperplaters offered another: "Resolved, by this most august body of the world's toilers now in session that we extend to the sufferers of Russia our condolence and sympathy, and, furthermore, that this convention appropriate the . . . sum of one thousand dollars." Condolence and sympathy survived debate, but not the appropriation. Similarly, at the United Mine Workers' convention, a motion was made "to take up a collection to be sent to the Russian working men. . . . The motion was seconded but not carried."[25]

Farmers, reading their magazines in early 1905, must have been reminded of the fist-shaking Populism of the 1890s. "We weep for the butchered peasants," the *California Cultivator* said, "fertilizing with their blood the land which they had sought to make their own." *Kansas Farmer* congratulated the courageous assassins who had taken the lives of Plehve and the Grand Duke Sergius. "It takes a farmer to be a real man," it declared. National-circulation papers such as *Farmer's Review* and *American Agriculturist* also displayed pride that leading terrorists were all from the SR peasants' movement. The only way to get the job done, the national *Homestead* suggested, was to "kill a few hundred of the leading nobles as quickly as possible." Language remained constant in tone during the shift of 1905. Farm editors still encouraged mayhem, but targets were different. "Russia's urban radicals who incline to violence must be wiped out," said the *Kansas Farmer*. It was also clear, Seth Bottomly wrote in *Farm, Stock, and Home,* another national monthly, that bloodthirsty Jews, not peasants, were causing present disturbances in Russia. Jews were responsible—as well as vodka, a convenient starting point for prohibition tirades in the *Kansas Farmer,* a paper that contributed the curious observation that all vodka breweries were run by Jews. At other times, when the *Farmer* reckoned that all Jews and revolutionaries were socialists, it came much closer to representing journalism's major theme of late 1905.[26]

It was true enough that socialists of various factions were involved in the movement to overthrow the Tsar. But roles played by liberals remained equally important. Men who were devoting their careers to the study of Russia, such as George Kennan and Samuel Harper, referred repeatedly to the revolution's complexity and insisted that its political outcome was unpredictable. Popular journalists did not agree. "Americans are not in-betweeners," the *Chicago News* firmly stated.[27] From the ashes of one oversimplification rose another. Excessive admiration gave way to excessive abuse, sustained by moralistic considerations no less galvanic than those of six months before. Once described as stalwart and virtuous fighters for freedom, Russians were now depicted as waving red flags and shouting Marxist slogans during orgies of arson, murder, and rape. The revolution's latest importance to journalists apparently lay in its ability to provide colorful examples of what might well happen at home unless Americans remained sternly vigilant.

American socialism was on the move, giving adversaries some reason for apprehension. In the presidential election of 1904, over four hundred thousand had voted for Eugene V. Debs and his Socialist party, four times the number of votes the party received in 1900. Party membership was growing, and circulation of its best-known publication, *Appeal to Reason,* sometimes reached three million for special issues. Scare stories described the formation of two new socialist organizations in 1905. Vigorous membership drives made a startling success of Bill Haywood's Industrial Workers of the World. At the same time Upton Sinclair and Jack London toured the nation's campuses, setting up chapters of their Intercollegiate Socialist Society. Daniel DeLeon stubbornly kept his Socialist Labor party separate from the general movement. He thought of his organization as exclusive and elite but was proud of its popularity too, proved by the alleged fact that he had to turn away hundreds of applicants of the Debs sort, sentimentalists who did not really understand Karl Marx.

"There is no question that thousands of well-meaning citizens have become enamored of socialistic remedies," the president of the National Association of Manufacturers, David M. Parry, told a convention audience. He moved smoothly into detailed accounts of atrocities by Russian revolutionaries, displaying not the smallest doubt that these belonged in a speech on the dangers of socialism at home. The press, both general and special, spoke of twin terrors. As the pro-Roosevelt *Square Deal* commented, socialism was un-American whether "manifest in St. Petersburg or New York City." The main purpose of drawing such parallels was to harm American radicalism, but the *Toledo Socialist,* seeing that damages would be reciprocal, apologized to the Russian revolution.[28]

While membership figures showed that socialists were going strong, their direction was anything but certain, and they were more a menace to themselves than to capitalism. Intramural fights left little time for worry over Russia's revolution, even were it possible to agree that it deserved socialist support.

The Socialist Labor party, contemptuous of other socialists and proud of an elite reputation, restricted membership to applicants who could display knowledge of dialectical materialism and historical inevitability. Party leader DeLeon interpreted Marx in the strictest sense, certain that successful proletarian revolution could occur only after a society had reached an advanced stage of capitalism. Therefore, while working to overthrow bourgeois capitalism at home, DeLeon hoped for the triumph of this same system over Tsarist feudalism. The present revolution annoyed him. Historical inevitability must work in orderly fashion, but how could it when capitalists, peasants, and proletarians insisted upon breaking their chains concurrently? DeLeon criticized the "dumbness" of proletarians who marched to their deaths on Bloody Sunday. The gesture had been in vain, he said, and the fact that a priest had led them commented upon the ridiculous nature of the entire revolution. Socialist Labor's chief publication, the *Weekly People*, ignored Russia for the better part of 1905.[29]

DeLeon and his comrades viewed the much larger Socialist party as practically useless, awkward in size and incoherent in purpose. One of its biographers has written that "the Socialist Party in its heyday was composed of a little of everything–of recent immigrants and descendants of the *Mayflower*'s passengers, of tenement dwellers and prairie farmers, of intellectuals and unlettered sharecroppers, of devout ministers and belligerent agnostics, of syndicalists and craft unionists, of revolutionists and gradualist reformers." Party members accused one another of anti-Semitism, and fought over whether to segregate the party's Negro members at conventions. Catholics refused to work with those who said that God and socialism were incompatible. Native-born socialists sometimes behaved like Daughters of the American Revolution in their attitudes toward immigrant comrades. The latter, still calling themselves sds, srs, and *Bundists* in the European manner, were occupied with arguments they had brought with them to America—menshevism versus bolshevism, terrorism versus gradualism, and patriotism versus internationalism. Comrades who were farmers and laborers resented the influence of those whom William Z. Foster called the nonproletarian intellectuals—Victor Berger and Algie Simons in Milwaukee; Morris Hilquit, Gaylord Wilshire, and William E. Walling's University Settlement clique in New York; as well as Upton Sinclair, Jack London, Thorstein Veblen, and Clarence Darrow on the college lecture circuit. The intellectuals had taken over the major publications and made them, as one member complained to Hilquit, "too scholarly for the average socialist readers." Their arguments were spirited if scholarly, and they included the issue of the Russian revolution. It was not a socialist movement, *Wilshire's Magazine* said, for the mental horizon of its leaders was "not much broader than that of an intelligent Texas steer." Eugene V. Debs agreed, saying the revolution was violent, terroristic, undisciplined, and lacked sufficient proletarian involvement. It was a typically liberal revolution, and Debs wanted nothing to do with it. Much opposed to Debs were London, Walling, Poole, and others, who were proving themselves capable of shrugging off dull doctrines which threatened to spoil the romance of overthrowing tyranny.[30]

Despite bickering, all organizations set up fund-raising committees. Socialist Labor had collected only $128.57 by the end of April 1905, and thereafter the *Weekly People* did not bother to report figures. When the iww was organized in

June, delegates in Chicago's Brand Hall heard a rousing speech that pledged "financial assistance . . . to our persecuted comrades in far-off Russia." There was no response, but later Bill Haywood sent in three dollars. The Socialist party, so undisciplined that many of its members could work for the revolution free from philosophical rumination, was more successful. Hilquit, London, and others formed the American Friends of the Russian Revolution, a money-raising organization which took in more than five thousand dollars by the end of the year, the bulk of this contributed during November and December.[31]

Like other Americans, socialists were changing their minds during the latter half of 1905. Regard for the revolution seemed to grow with each new evidence that middle-class Americans were no longer tainting it with their own approval. More important was news of massive industrial strikes, occurring in St. Petersburg in October and Moscow in December. Russian workers, assumed to be SDs, at last were getting the headlines instead of Miliukov and his liberals. Socialist editors began to apologize for having doubted the proletarian nature of the revolution. Even DeLeon came to believe that it might be possible to overthrow feudalism and capitalism at the same time, hoping that the Russian workers, in their untutored groping, might accidentally open the door to Marx's final stage of history. Russia made page one of the *Weekly People* when DeLeon called for a nation-wide demonstration to take place on the first anniversary of Bloody Sunday.[32]

January 22, 1906, the New York *Worker* said, was "the grandest day in American socialism's courageous support of its Russian comrades." Members of all parties, thirty-five thousand strong, linked arms in a parade that ventured far beyond the boundaries of New York's East Side. Chicago's gray and slushy streets were brightened by hundreds of red banners waving over the heads of marchers. In Milwaukee, Cincinnati, Detroit, Philadelphia, Pittsburgh, St. Louis, and

San Francisco, crowds sang the "Internationale" and hoisted signs which bore a variety of slogans: "Hurrah for the Revolution," "Russians Arise," "There are Two Revolutions," "Together We Break Our Chains."[33]

This type of activity did not please Russian revolutionists. They possessed slogans enough already, and most assuredly could not welcome support that might frighten away the last of their other American friends—those with money.

Witte

6. We Should Not Have Come Here

SERGEI WITTE'S VICTORIES in America pleased Nicholas as much as they distressed revolutionaries. In the weeks that followed, with the first trainloads of soldiers arriving from Manchuria, liberals did not believe that even the token parliament, promised before the government heard the news from Portsmouth, would become a reality. On the day of his arrival in St. Petersburg, Witte spent several hours with the Tsar, presenting details of all accomplishments—peace without a crippling indemnity, alteration of American public opinion, and preliminary arrangements for a Morgan loan as well as for numerous other business investments in Russia. "I told him of his new honor," Nicholas wrote later. "I am creating him a Count. He went quite stiff with emotion and then tried three times to kiss my hand."[1]

The reunion was not all that it might have been, for the emperor seemed depressed and nervous, often failing to disguise his impatience as the diplomat rambled on. Practically all of Russia was on strike. Witte had seen some results of this shortly after his disembarkation at the Neva River docks. Except for mounted Cossacks, out in force, the streets were deserted. Droshkies parked outside hotel entrances lacked horses and drivers. Doors were padlocked on trolleys that stood in rows along the Nevsky Prospect.

Troubles had snowballed from a demand for higher wages by Moscow typographical workers. St. Petersburg printers were first to join the walkout, which then spread to industries of all kinds in cities throughout the country. "No political party had foreseen it or planned it," an SD official reluctantly admitted. "It broke out suddenly . . . as a spark strikes a dry leaf and from it the wind carries millions of sparks to set new fires." Peasants rose in rebellion. Induced more by famine than by SR orators, they burned landlords' houses and captured food supplies. The St. Petersburg Soviet (name given a central strike committee which at that time had no special political connection) demanded that food be shipped to critical areas. Impossible, came the answer from the Ministry of Interior, for there was not a train running anywhere in Russia. Ministerial propagandists, resorting to bluff, issued daily reminders that the general strike was hurting the people far more than the government. But Nicholas was not so sure about this. Advised to shrug his shoulders and show casual unconcern in the presence of visitors, he wrote that he was really "sick . . . to read the news. . . . One had the same feeling as before a thunderstorm in summer. . . . The ministers, instead of acting with quick decision, only assemble in council like a lot of frightened hens." He was grateful to General Trepov, who "made it quite plain to the populace that . . . disorder would be ruthlessly put down." The Tsar fully approved when Trepov ordered Cossacks not to spare the cartridges.[2]

Bloodshed only made matters worse. Droshky and trolley drivers joined the strike, as did doctors, professors, telegraphers, and, in the Tsar's words, "every kind of riffraff." There were riots in several army regiments, and Nicholas was forced to employ his most dependable troops, the Seme-novsky Guards, to put down a mutiny of twelve hundred sailors at Kronstadt, the island naval base in the mouth of the Neva. St. Petersburg's nights were pitch black following a walkout of municipal electrical workers. Strikers milled about in the streets, keeping well away from bonfires tended by police at important intersections, and making their way from one candlelit meeting to another in order to listen to competing politicians clamor for their allegiance.[3]

SRS and SDS at first had counseled against a general strike, because it was much too suggestive of union tactics in democratic countries in that it sought shop improvements rather than political change. The parties grew interested only after Trepov's bullets improved chances that their talented orators might be able to turn the strike into a march on the Winter Palace.

As far as American socialists were concerned, the strike was political from start to finish. Social Democrats had engineered it, the *Worker* assumed. Abraham Cahan, exuberant as ever, proclaimed in a *Daily Forward* headline, "Workers with Red Flag in Hand Free Russia." It was clear that socialism had gained ascendancy over all other factions, the *Toledo Socialist* asserted. Emma Goldman, who had favored SRS, no longer worried about the relative prominence of peasants and workers in the movement. News of the strike, she wrote, was "electrifying and carried us to ecstatic heights." She said that the East Side "lived in a delirium, spending almost all of its time at monster meetings and discussing these matters in cafés, forgetting political differences and brought into close comradeship by the glorious events happening in the fatherland."[4]

"Heavens, what a time they are having in Russia," Theodore Roosevelt exclaimed without exceptional regret. News of strikes and other evidently radical activities convinced him anew that he had acted rightly in opposing the revolution. Those same events presented the press with its first good chance to prove that the mood of early 1905 had been a misplaced infatuation. The *New York Herald* severely criticized journalists who at one time had grossly exaggerated the unhappy condition of the Russian people and portrayed the Tsar in a disparaging manner. The *Herald*'s editors revealed that they had felt, even in February, that their colleagues were making a terrible mistake. The *Independent*, too, said it had suspected all along that the revolution would turn out to be socialistic. Papers which had once praised revolutionaries now called them radicals, communists, extremists, anarchists, nihilists, homosexuals, rowdies, and Jacobins. The fight for freedom had been transformed into a terrible curse, journalists said, a reign of terror similar to the bloodiest days of the French Revolution. The strike only proved, said many writers, that Russians were disinclined to work, lacked character, had no respect for law, and were absolutely unfit for self-government. The *Nation* advised the Tsar to adopt tougher policies: "The whiff of grapeshot will do the business, and do it with the approval of the civilized world and of all in Russia who have property." The press also showed grave concern for those men who in good faith had departed on business trips to Russia, only to be confronted by the Red Terror.[5]

Spencer Eddy, chargé d'affaires in St. Petersburg, spent hours of his time in the United States Embassy's best carriage, one with golden eagles in bas-relief on the doors. Thinking the revolution had ended with Portsmouth, Ambassador Meyer had returned to America for what he described as a well-earned vacation. It was Eddy's task, almost every day it seemed, to meet important businessmen at gangways or railway stations and convey them to the embassy for conferences and entertainment. Travelers spoke with surprise of the unsettled look of things as they peered through carriage windows. Eddy informed them of the great strike which was spreading throughout the country. Some were frightened, while others showed contempt for dangers. Many were displeased with Witte, saying that he had hoodwinked them concerning the true state of affairs in Russia. Later, when they conferred with the count, he assured them that he too had been astonished when he had returned to find the revolution not yet suppressed. One must make the best of temporary discomforts, he said, stating that the strikers were starving and could not possibly hold out much longer. Secretary of State Root cabled Eddy that he must protect the businessmen by all means at his command, sheltering them in the embassy if necessary. As it turned out, most visitors preferred to live in the Singer Sewing Machine Company, a modern building of granite and steel construction. There W. E. Smith of Westinghouse sponsored memorable parties and became the acknowledged social leader of the colony.[6]

The streets were safe in daytime, allowing excursions to the golf course in the Finnish Village as well as business errands to the palace and the ministries. The Tsar's English was good enough to allow him to say "splendid" as each plan was explained to him. John Wanamaker, of Rockefeller's Standard Oil, offered to replace all equipment destroyed during the strike in the Baku oilfields. Dozens of candles illuminated the emperor's conference with Smith of Westinghouse, who pointed out St. Petersburg's need for new generators and other electrical equipment. "Splendid," Nicholas said, when James J. Hill's emissary told him not to worry about the Bering Straits, suggesting that trains running from New York to St. Petersburg could use ferry boats until the tunnel was ready. The *Washington Post* said cynically, "Who wants to go to St. Petersburg?" But Robert T. Grass, of the American Locomotive Company, gave unqualified support and offered to provide a ceremonial golden spike on the day of the line's completion. Despite the revolution, sales of reapers and plows were gaining, and McCormick's agent advertised for steady young Russians, who wanted to get ahead, to work in new branches planned for Siberia and the Ukraine. The Singer Company also wanted to increase the number of its agencies. Recent hardships had not prevented Russians from keeping up their sewing machine payments, and few repossessions had been reported.[7]

Count Witte encouraged all projects, assuring everyone that Russia's credit was as solid as Pittsburgh steel due to the foreign loan that would be signed almost any day. In addition, he said, his nation was rich in resources and soon would enter a period of unparalleled prosperity. Quoting Witte extensively, the *American Exporter* predicted dramatic changes in the Russian way of life and analyzed market prospects in telephones, automobiles, bathtubs, stuffed animals, and musical instruments.[8]

For the time being, Russia's best market was in munitions, the demand for which had been affected but little by the end of the Japanese war. Earlier in the year, Charles M. Schwab of Bethlehem Steel had proposed to build a fleet of battleships to replace those now lying at the bottom of the Sea of Japan. After disagreement over prices, he had returned to Pittsburgh with no more than a million dollar contract for armor plate. Charles R. Flint, presently free-lancing, arrived with a bargain for the Tsar. Having been authorized to sell obsolete Chilean and Argentinian warships, Flint described his wares as almost like new, six vessels for a bargain rate of thirty-five million dollars. The price was splendid, Nicholas admitted, but in the end he declined the offer. His current needs were more in the line of rifles, machine guns, and light artillery. Flint said that he could supply these at great savings. Competition was rugged, for salesmen from Krupp, Armstrong, Schneider-Creusot, and Skoda also had been drawn to St. Petersburg by news of riots and strikes. The American held his own so well that his advertising methods and liberal credit offers were subjects of official complaints by the German consul. Flint returned to New York with books filled with orders. How many he actually placed with manufacturers is uncertain due to his increasing worries about Russian solvency.[9]

Because they were offering credit, American salesmen paid

close attention to every rumor from the Ministry of Finance, where bankers were holding daily consultations. They speculated about when the loan would be signed, and what its size would be. Most bets were on two hundred and fifty or two hundred and sixty million dollars, but some believed three hundred million dollars was possible. Any of these amounts ought to see the Tsar safely through the revolution, which was costing five million dollars per month to suppress, and maintain Russian credit for some time to come. During the last two weeks of October, the House of Morgan representatives, George Perkins and J. P. Morgan, Jr., held long sessions at the Ministry, and these implied that settlement was imminent. Competitors were on the scene. Finance Minister V. N. Kokovtsev had employed an American, Judge Charles Mayer, to plead the Tsar's case in a number of European capitals, and Mayer had been able to bring to St. Petersburg a representative from Barings of London; Messrs. Netzlin and Bronson of the Banque de Paris and Crèdit Lyonaise; Baron Hottinguer of Bleichraeders in Berlin; and other bankers from Amsterdam and Berne.[10]

Crudely printed handbills saying, "Do not lend money to the Tsar," found their way into the Singer Sewing Machine Company, where they were carefully folded and saved by Americans who wanted to take home souvenirs of their dangerous journey. Most prized were tracts that bore the printed signature of Maxim Gorky. Revolutionaries had been issuing such warnings for months, threatening that the Tsar's downfall was certain and that this would mean repudiation of all his debts. Now they increased their efforts, protesting against "foreign bankers . . . advancing money to the present government to maintain its grip at the very throat of the people." They had no real hope of influencing French and German financiers but could not believe that Morgan and Perkins would "advance American money to perpetuate the existing regime."[11]

It was hardly sentimentality that was causing the two

Americans to question the wisdom of their mission. The handbills, pathetic enough in themselves, served to call more attention to the general strike, which had already produced a distinctly unhealthy atmosphere for loan negotiations. As always, Count Witte was reassuring. The Russian people love the Tsar, he told Morgan, and the strike was the work of a mere handful of anarchists.[12]

Ignoring the European bankers, the Americans conferred privately with Witte and Finance Minister Kokovtsev. Several weeks before, on the Hudson River, J. P. Morgan, Sr., had promised Witte that he would extend to the Tsar all the money he needed—from two hundred and fifty to three hundred and fifty million dollars—and there would be no need to deal with any other banking house. In return, Morgan's men now revealed, he required a pledge that Russia would never borrow from Schiff's or any other Jewish house in New York; that Russia must allow Morgan to handle all her business in the United States; and that she grant empire sales monopolies to American steel, farm equipment, and products of other industries in which Morgan held interests.[13] The last demand, if accepted, would practically destroy Russia's trade relations with Britain, Germany, and more importantly France, a faithful friend and subsidizer in recent years.

A crestfallen Witte left the decision to Kokovtsev, who quickly declined the proposition. The minister told Morgan that he desired close trade relations with the United States but did not believe in going to extremes. He walked down the hall to a room where the Europeans waited. They had implied a willingness to loan Russia money on terms much less severe than those of Morgan.[14]

The American bankers showed little dismay over Kokovtsev's decision, because it had, in all likelihood, saved them from embarrassment. In the end, considering their rapidly growing concern for Russia's future, they probably would have withdrawn their offer to take all of the bonds. Now they joined the European group and staked claim to a fifty million dollar piece of the issue. They were even more modest two days later. The House of Morgan would be satisfied with just twenty million dollars, even though Netzlin and Hottinguer were more than willing to assign a larger portion to the Americans. The sound of distant small arms fire seemed out of place on what eventually proved to be a most gracious and unselfish day in the history of international finance.[15]

The United States Embassy reported: "Quite naturally the bankers do not desire to place any money in the hands of a government which may possibly cease to exist during the next few months. Mr. George W. Perkins and Mr. J. Pierpont Morgan, Jr., . . . seem to be entirely in accord with their colleagues, and it is probable that unless the strikes cease and order is once more restored, the efforts of the government to negotiate a loan at the present moment will fail."[16]

Kokovtsev was suddenly frantic to unload his bonds. A real killing was possible for anyone with courage enough to buy up temporarily unwanted goods. But first it would be necessary to get inside information on revolutionary prospects.

Sergei Petrov, a prominent Social Democrat and a member of the student council at St. Petersburg University, was surprised by a visit from a *London Times* correspondent who had been looking for a revolutionary who spoke English and had heard that Petrov fulfilled these qualifications. "A friend of mine would be delighted to meet you," the correspondent told Petrov. "He is a very important person in his country."[17]

At the appointed hour Petrov was admitted to the correspondent's apartment on the Nevsky Prospect. He had never seen such luxury, he wrote later. He was introduced to "an overdressed young man with blond hair and blue eyes." Petrov understood that this was one of the notorious

American bankers even though the young man gave no name, saying that he preferred to remain incognito. The Russian could appreciate the need for secrecy, the name Petrov being an alias he had used for several months.

The American spoke of a rumor he had heard that if the Reds came to power they would not pay the debts of the present government. "I cannot believe this," he said. "Moreover, I do not believe they will ever get power." "Wait and see," Petrov replied.

"The press makes much of your meetings," the banker went on, "but I have been assured by high—yes, very high—authorities that all you have there is a handful of anarchists and students. The people—the peasants and the workers—are firmly behind the throne."

"Come to our meeting and check this information."

"How can I? Won't the anarchists kill me?"

"I guarantee your complete safety," Petrov said. "Come to the university tonight. I will keep a place for you."

As he later admitted, Petrov staged a kind of meeting best calculated to terrify "the arrogant young man." The latter, accompanied by four business associates, entered the student council hall at eight o'clock sharp. The Americans were dressed identically in black overcoats and yellow kid gloves. All seemed nervous, frowning at curious students who surrounded them. Spying their host, they shook hands "with such profusion of cordiality" that Petrov was embarrassed, fearing other students would think that they were his "very, very dear friends." There were catcalls from the crowd while the Americans were shown to chairs on the speakers' platform.

Petrov delivered a short lecture on the imminent victory of revolution, then sat beside his guests in order to translate other speeches. Comrade Nikolai described the gory fate awaiting the anointed butcher in the Winter Palace. Comrade Krylenko was next, choosing as his topic the interference of foreign capitalists in Russian affairs.

"The emissaries of foreign banks are here, in St. Petersburg," Krylenko shouted, pivoting and thrusting a finger at the wide-eyed delegation behind him. "Do they believe that their dollars will change the course of the revolution and give the despots a new lease on life? Comrades, will you let these vultures make money by ganging up with the enemies of the Russian people?"

"Never, never," roared the audience.

"We should not have come here," one of the Americans whispered.

Krylenko continued: "The revolution will triumph over its enemies. The foreign capitalistic sharks will come to us with their claims, showing the note signed—in blood—by the Tsar. What answer will you give them, comrades?"

The deafening response, the hundreds of waving fists, prompted the guests to rise from their chairs. "We have heard enough," they said. "Please help us to get away from here before it is too late."

Petrov led them out of the hall. They muttered, "Dreadful, dreadful," while he escorted them a safe distance away from the university.

"So this is what is going on here," one said.

"It is the same in all the colleges," Petrov told them.

"Dreadful," said the blond young man. "One can't keep far enough away from this mess. We are deeply obliged to you." After another round of handshaking, Petrov returned to the university.

On the next morning, October 30, the American embassy learned that there definitely would be no loan to the Tsar. J. P. Morgan, Jr., George Perkins, and four business associates, had departed suddenly from the city. "They expect to return at a later date," a somewhat euphemistic dispatch stated, "when such negotiations can be carried on with more security." The *New York Times* described a wild carriage ride to the Neva docks. Perkins said later that he and Morgan had sensed no fear, but he could not deny that he had tried to charter the German liner *Darmstadt* for fifteen thousand dollars. The vessel was not due to sail for another three days, and its captain refused to alter the schedule. Reuters reported the bankers on the island of Kronstadt, under protection of the Imperial Navy, and an Associated Press bulletin placed the armored cruiser *Minneapolis* in the Baltic, steaming at full speed to the rescue. Persistent efforts to charter a ship brought a welcome telegram from the captain of the Russian cattleboat *Oihouna*, then in Helsinki. In what was probably the most profitable voyage of his career, he picked up his passengers on the evening of November 1 and deposited them in Stockholm two days later.[18]

Morgan and Perkins sailed from Russia on the day the strike ended, the result of an Imperial manifesto promising reforms. Of necessity the promises were more extensive than those contained in four other manifestos issued within the past year. There would be civil liberties—inviolability of person; freedom of conscience, speech, and assembly; and the right to form unions. There would be a Duma with real legislative powers, its members to be chosen by universal suffrage. Joy among liberals was unrestrained. Miliukov completed work on his new political organization, proudly naming it the Constitutional Democratic party. Other factions watched and waited. The St. Petersburg Soviet, lately controlled by a coalition of SRs and SDs, agreed to call off the strike but was prepared to renew it pending the turn of events.

Nicholas was disturbed by the scope of his promises. Only two weeks earlier he had desired to appoint a military dictator who would crush the rebellion by sheer force. No one had wanted the job. "If he wants to force me to become Dictator," said one of the prime candidates, "I shall kill myself in his presence with this revolver." Moreover, the Tsar was learning that Cossack tactics were ineffective against strikers. Riots could be broken by force, as Trepov was proving almost every day in the streets of the capital, but he could do nothing about men who hid in their houses and refused to come to work. Reluctantly, the Tsar turned to an opposite alternative, one which Witte had been advocating since his return from America. The count's program included the creation of a new office of prime minister, which he himself would occupy, and the announcement of reforms of such magnitude as to end the strike and perhaps the revolution as well. Nicholas comprehended what Witte had in mind, but even pretended surrender was distasteful to him. He delayed for as long as he could, then crossed himself three times and signed the manifesto that Witte had prepared. Later, kneeling beside an infuriated Alexandra, he asked God's forgiveness for betraying his coronation oath, the memory of his father, obligations to his infant son, and the principle of divine right.[19]

Premier Witte, loyal to the same principle, now concentrated on the job of preserving it through devices he considered superior to those of Trepov. "I have a constitution in my head," he told an English visitor, "but as to my heart" —and he spat on the floor.[20] The Founding Father, as some American papers called him, gave assurances that he was already hard at work on the job of writing the constitution. Liberal leaders, who had expected to share this burden, were immediately suspicious—feelings entirely justified, as they would learn a few months later when they read Witte's final draft. He rendered universal suffrage harmless with ingenious electoral mechanisms designed to assure a highly conservative Duma. There were fundamental laws with which legislators must not tamper, nor were they judged competent to debate any question touching on war, foreign policy, or finance. On the off chance that some future Duma might prove bothersome, the few activities allowed it were made subject to veto by a state council, in large part appointive by the Tsar. There were also provisions for special administrative decrees, for declarations of states of emergency during which the constitution would be suspended, and for the Duma's dismissal whenever the Tsar wished.

While the manifesto's promises would turn out to be worthless, its issuance was important to government public relations both at home and abroad. Witte understood this importance, and it was one of the reasons he had advised the Tsar to choose conciliation instead of repressive measures which might again turn, he said, "the whole civilized world against the Russian government." He had worked diligently in America, establishing good relations, and these needed careful tending. Shortly after the appearance of the manifesto, he sent greetings to the United States: "I am sure the American people who understand what freedom is, and the American press which voices the wish of the people, will rejoice that . . . the Russian people have received from his Imperial Majesty the promises and the guarantees of freedom, and will join in the hope that the Russian people will wisely . . . cooperate with the government for their peaceful introduction. . . . It is necessary to respect the ideals of the great majority of society and not the views of noisy groups and factions, too often unstable."[21]

Any rejoicing evident in America was more in behalf of the leaders than the Russian people. "The Emperor Nicholas and Count Witte are the men of the hour," *Farmer's Guide* said. They were Russia's Washington and Lincoln in the opinion of the *Tampa Tribune*. The *Chicago Tribune* admired the way Witte was getting things done and recalled its August prediction that he would rise to the top. "The visit to America has inspired him," the *Watchman* said; and the *Christian Advocate* also held that he had written the manifesto and would write a constitution "with the memory of free America fresh in his mind." A *Saturday Evening Post* article, "The United States of Muscovy," told how Americanization of the world was becoming a reality. Even the usually astute *New York Times* praised the count's accomplishment, which it held to be the result of democratic convictions acquired during his recent sojourn in America. Insight was rare among the press, but not totally absent. "It don't seem to amount to much," *Painter and Decorator*, a labor monthly published in Lafayette, Indiana, said of the manifesto.[22]

Other editors, no matter how much they admired Witte as a person, believed that he had made a mistake in carrying American ideals too far. Russians simply were not ready for all that the manifesto would give them, said the *Detroit News*, formerly a strong admirer of Miliukov's liberals. The *World Today* believed self-rule to be "out of the question in a nation with millions of ignorant peasants." These people must be satisfied with smaller gains, the *Christian Advocate* suggested, "pending their future mental and moral development." The *Chicago Tribune* advised revolutionaries to get down on their knees and thank the Tsar for having given them much more than they deserved. The *Coast Seamen's Journal* protested, "It has probably never occurred to any of these highly superior organs of respectable mediocrity that the only way in which a people can fit themselves for self-government is by practicing it."[23]

American Jews puzzled over the meaning of Witte's latest enterprise. Their newspapers gave special attention to the manifesto's civil rights clause. It did not specifically eliminate Jews as had the Easter ukase. Yet the wording of the clause was suspiciously vague. Some commentators were hopeful, while others could have no confidence in any of Witte's works.[24] Debates between optimists and pessimists had hardly begun when they were settled abruptly by news from Russia.

Nicholas II

7. The Pogrom

THE POGROMS of November 1905, were the worst in Russia's history. They began on the day the manifesto was announced, and for that reason were said to be an integral part of Witte's program of concessions to the Russian people. While the premier did nothing to stop the massacres, he insisted that he had not known about them in advance. His enemies in the Ministry of Interior made no such denials. They had detested the manifesto plan, believing that even counterfeit concessions would encourage dangerous modes of thought among the population. Now was the perfect time to teach another sort of lesson, especially to those people likely to be most joyous over Witte's promises. General Trepov and other Interior officials had known what was coming, welcomed it, and would do all that they could to enhance its effectiveness.

As usual, organizational details were handled by the patriotic societies known collectively as the Black Hundreds. (The Tsar was proud to include their ribbons and badges among his full-dress decorations, and similar ornaments were prized as symbols of social respectability by conservative-minded bureaucrats, policemen, and businessmen.) Committees worked busily during the month of October. Some transported barrels of vodka to private homes, schoolhouses, and other points selected as distribution centers. Others cranked out handbills by the millions, saying that Jews were foreigners, not true Russians; and that they were cheating people, causing children to starve and fomenting all troubles. "Put an end to them in the real Russian way," said one handbill. The Church was happy to be of service, spreading the message through a chain letter project: "Each person who receives this letter must make at least three copies and send them to other villages and towns. He who has not fulfilled this order within six days will be stricken by grave sickness and affliction, but whoever spreads more than three copies of this letter will be granted recovery from incurable diseases and prosperity in all things." Some committees worked door to door, asking about religious affiliation and reminding Christians to paint white crosses on the fronts of their houses. It was ordered that this work be done at twilight on November 1, so Jews would not be given advance warning of what would befall them that night.[1]

General Trepov grew careless, boasting openly that the St. Petersburg pogrom would be a great success, and publishing lists of persons marked for death. Revolutionary parties in the capital were well organized and proudly aware that Cossacks had failed to defeat them during the general strike. They warned Trepov that they would stand together and fight the Black Hundreds. The general backed down. There was no pogrom in St. Petersburg, but Jews were not so fortunate in six hundred and sixty other communities. Odessa suffered most with over seven hundred killed, thousands injured, and some forty thousand ruined through destruction of their property. Throughout the nation about three thousand lost their lives during the first week of November, and property losses came to over thirty-one million dollars. In contrast with earlier pogroms, Jews in some cities fought back. There were reports of men and women defending their homes with rocks and kitchen knives—actions that only heightened the wrath of mobs and incurred the active participation of policemen and soldiers who, under normal pogrom conditions, usually had been content to stand and watch.[2]

The writer Sholem Aleichem sent a cable to a friend in New York City. He described the Jewish community in Kiev as totally destroyed. Thousands were homeless and starving. "Arouse the public and make a great appeal for help," he urged.[3]

The response was incredible, *Menorah* said—the most remarkable Jewish gathering ever held in the United States. No one was surprised to see banker Jacob Schiff, eyes streaming tears, throw his arms around socialist editor Abraham Cahan at the Temple Emanu-El, which was the scene of a laughing, crying, back-pounding reunion of Germans and Russians, orthodox and agnostics, and socialists and Wall Street millionaires. Conservative and radical papers agreed that the immensity of the pogrom had welded diverse groups together in a manner previously considered impossible. "At last, for the first time, it has really happened," the *Israelite* declared, "a sense of unity among American Jews."[4]

There were daily meetings at the temple. Schiff found himself on nine committees and fourteen subcommittees. Money had to be raised, and that meant publicity campaigns, parades, hiring halls for rallies and theaters for benefit performances. The first parades got out of hand. Sometimes there were four or five in a single night, dismaying police by the way they moved at random through the East Side, producing good-natured riots whenever they intersected. The temple alliance began to impose control upon the marchers, and police reported perfect behavior on November 24, when over one hundred thousand people, chanting prayers and moaning in eerie harmony, walked the length of Broadway. American Jews hoped that the parades and other demonstrations would call attention to the fund drives. Boxes and buckets had been placed on every East Side street corner, as well as in drugstores and saloons. These filled rapidly with pennies, nickels, and dimes, despite numerous thefts blamed on Irishmen and Italians.[5]

Schiff sent four hundred telegrams in an effort to unify campaigns throughout the nation. The first outburst of enthusiasm had produced over a dozen collection committees in New York City alone, and Schiff was treasurer of half of these. As the days passed he was able to bring into being an amalgamation called the National Committee for Relief of Sufferers by Russian Massacres.

Schiff's personal check was for fifty thousand dollars. Contributions from Oscar Straus, Cyrus Sulzberger, Daniel Guggenheim, Adolph Lewisohn, and Simon Wolf were almost as generous. In Philadelphia's Mercantile Hall, Judge Mayer Sulzberger presided over a rally where twenty thousand dollars were collected within half an hour. Competition developed. The Plum Street Temple in Cincinnati reported five thousand dollars raised in only four minutes. Schiff's national committee received slightly over a half million from out-of-town sources, and New York did even better. The city's total on November 17, for example, was $76,912, much of it in small change from the East Side. This figure was surpassed the following day at a benefit performance of tragic readings featuring Sarah Bernhardt and Mark Twain. By the end of November, Schiff had over a million dollars to send to the *Hilfsverein der deutschen Juden,* an organization that possessed means for smuggling rubles into Russia. The final figure, when the drive ended in January, was $1,217,695.[6]

The *New York Times* inspired contributions by printing daily collection totals and encouraging editorials. Here was proof, it said repeatedly, that Americans still cared for those who suffered oppression in foreign lands. The sacred heritage was not dead. Never in the history of the world had so much money been raised for relief, at least through means of popular subscription.

Editorials in the *Times* also revealed growing concern that contribution lists included few non-Jewish names. A ten thousand dollar check from Andrew Carnegie was welcomed with relief and special publicity. Carnegie specified that his gift was not to be used for revolutionary purposes. "Under the law of evolution," he wrote, "we must steadily, though slowly, march upward." J. P. Morgan, Sr., August Belmont, and Henry Clay Frick each sent in five thousand, and a hundred dollars arrived from Charles W. Fairbanks, vice-president of the United States. It was reported in the *Presbyterian* that "the Rev. R. B. Mattice, of the Throgg's Neck Presbyterian Church . . . alluded last Sabbath to the unhappy condition of these people and was agreeably surprised to find the offering amounted to thirty dollars." The remainder of the non-Jewish list, which included four Catholic archbishops and an equal number of Chinese tongs, was so short that the *Times* resorted to printing sympathy messages, unaccompanied by checks, from the Council of Churches of Christ, Wellesley College, the Indianapolis YMCA, the New York City Board of Aldermen, and the AFL (once again Gompers' union had voted down a motion to send money). The *Times* at last admitted that "the Christian response was disappointing," accounting for less than five percent of the total raised. While the paper frequently referred to this poor showing, it was careful not to scold. Publisher Adolph Ochs was a Jew, and the *Sun* and the *Herald* never lost a chance to accuse their rival of bias in pogrom coverage.[7]

In the early days of the campaign, before its success was assured, sponsors resorted to extreme measures in attempting to persuade all Americans to contribute. They announced that all money going to Russia would be distributed on a nonpartisan basis. It would go to Christians, even those who had taken part in pogroms, as well as to Jews. And not one penny would go for revolutionary purposes, the fund raisers promised. Socialists protested this policy, but only the *Bundists* dropped out of the Temple Emanu-El alliance. Nor did businessman Cyrus Sulzberger admire this evident need to show perfect behavior. "Jews should not actively solicit Christians," he said. "If they have to be begged, it's sad."⁸

At any rate, it became apparent as the drive continued, that begging would do no good. Attempting to understand American history, Jewish editors asked such questions as: What was wrong with people? Had ever there existed underdogs more helpless, more deserving of help? Had ever there occurred atrocities more fiendish? Had there been a more cynical chapter in the long history of monarchical rule? They assumed that the United States, being firmly dedicated to moral principles, had never before failed to respond to events such as those now taking place in Russia. Americans had helped French, Greeks, Germans, Hungarians, Irish, and Cubans. Editors wondered why Jews were an exception to the rule. "What did our people do," Cahan asked in the *Daily Forward*, "that such tragedy should befall it? How was it at fault that it evokes no response in the whole civilized world?"⁹

The rabbinate of Charlotte, North Carolina, condemned what it called the strange silence of the Christian clergy. In New York, Rabbi Joseph Silverman denounced the general press for not speaking out against the terrible pogrom. Referring to large newspapers and national magazines, the *Israelite* said, "Not one of them has a line which may be construed as expressing honest sympathy with the sadly afflicted Jews of Russia."¹⁰

The *Israelite* exaggerated only slightly. The *Times*, in its quiet way, was doing what it could, and William Randolph Hearst contributed the gaudy support of the *New York Evening Journal*, which called for millions of dollars for Russia's Hebrews as well as for immediate action by the United States government. Hearst recalled how he had created a war to free Cuba in 1898 and promised to do so again if necessary. This was no more than a cheap campaign trick, the *Herald* insinuated. The fact that Hearst was running for mayor of New York City, and needed the East Side vote, was prompting him to commit "outlandish breaches of journalistic good taste."[11]

Because of its sensation value, pogrom news dominated front pages during the first half of November. Casualty figures were multiplied by ten, and Associated Press teletypes disgorged dozens of eyewitness stories, giving full details on the appalling variety of methods that had been employed to end human life. Where editorial comment was concerned, the pogroms received scant attention. Some commentators, like correspondent Stanley Washburn of the *Chicago News,* said that Jews were responsible for what had happened, that they had been "squeezing everybody that came into their clutches and constantly fomenting trouble." They had driven the Tsar past the point of patient endurance, he said. Given the true circumstances, some editors wrote, Christians could not be expected to contribute to the relief fund, which would probably be spent for anarchy and assassination under the cloak of charity. Even if the cause were deserving, others wrote, the sending of aid would only anger the Tsar and make matters worse for the Jews. Racism, while certainly not to be admired, was a part of human nature, the *Christian Advocate* philosophized, saying that all the money in the world could not alter natural laws. *Vogue* counseled Jews not to "arouse more anti-Semitism toward themselves in America by making too much of an issue of it all."[12]

Papers that sympathized with pogrom victims often did so for the purpose of indicting the revolution on added counts. In committing beastly crimes, they said, the Russian people had proved beyond the shadow of a doubt that they were not fit to govern themselves. The *Houston Post* pointed to the latest terrors as proof that it had been correct all along in opposing the revolution. The *Chicago News* claimed that socialists had planned and carried out the pogroms.[13]

Most publications did not comment at all. This was understandable, the *Jewish Exponent* remarked cuttingly, for current miseries were poorly timed—the American heritage was not dead, it was only resting. The country frankly was bored by Russia's incorrigibility, its never-ending troubles, and was presently in the mood to avert its eyes from sorry spectacles, this paper said.[14]

Still another problem was complication, ancient tormentor of those who work in mass communications. Newspapermen had grown accustomed to being for the revolution, and then against it. It was difficult to choose sides when one revolutionary faction attacked another. Pogroms were "stale," said the editor of *Review of Reviews* as he explained why he was rejecting a story on the subject: "The situation in Russia is now so confused that it would be difficult, I fear, to select any clean-cut phase for treatment in an article."[15]

Prorevolutionary passions had failed to move government policy in early 1905. In November, with the press no longer interested, there was even less possibility of official interference in Russian affairs. Yet one could always hope. Telegrams and letters from Schiff, Straus, Wolf, and Cahan were among thousands sent to Washington by Jewish congregations, organizations, and community leaders. A few demanded war with Russia, while most politely suggested that humanitarian expressions by the president or Congress might persuade the Tsar to stop current pogroms earlier than otherwise might be expected.

Ambassador George Meyer, still on vacation in Boston, noted in his diary: "A Jewish delegation called on me and wanted to know if I would not urge the President to send a fleet to Russia with sealed orders. I refused as I said I consider it improper." The delegation also asked Meyer to use stern language when he saw the Tsar again, a suggestion equally unwelcome because it reminded him that he ought to be getting back to Russia.[16]

Meyer considered himself fortunate to have missed the October strike and was prepared to miss the pogroms as well. He had given Roosevelt a number of reasons for extending his leave—illness, family problems, and a Class of '79 dinner at Harvard. The president grew impatient. On November 6, he wired, "I think you should be in St. Petersburg now and that you ought not delay one day in starting." Three days later an even sharper message reprimanded Meyer for neglect of duty and ordered him to "get there at the earliest moment." Ten days later the ambassador called at the State Department for his instructions. He found Secretary Root in an aggravated mood, complaining about rich American Jews who were striving for notoriety. Schiff and Wolf, in their clamoring for the government to do something had put him on the spot. He had no intention, he said, of causing embarrassment by meddling in Russia's affairs. Yet he did not like being placed in the position of having to refuse publicly (Schiff would see that the Jewish press got hold of the story) to send a protest against events so immoral as the pogroms. Root told Meyer to explain this delicate matter to Count Witte, hoping that the resourceful premier could think of something to say "that would reassure and quiet . . . the influential Hebrews here."[17]

During a week's stopover in London, Meyer dropped in for a chat with Lord Lansdowne. The foreign secretary wholeheartedly agreed that there was no good reason for hurrying back to St. Petersburg and invited Meyer to remain in England for the rest of the hunting season. The idea was tempting, but Roosevelt was more to be feared than Russian turbulence. The ambassador moved on to Paris, where he took steps to ensure the safety of American diplomats in St. Petersburg. A cable requested that the cruiser *Minneapolis* be dispatched at once to the Russian capital. Following Root's refusal, Meyer arranged that four marines, attached to the Paris embassy, accompany him to his destination. He severely reprimanded an Associated Press reporter for sending out a story about the bodyguards. Reaching Berlin, Meyer dined with the Kaiser, bought two hundred cartridges for his rifle as well as two hundred rounds of number two buckshot, then began the last leg of his journey.[18]

Precautions were understandable. Meyer had received copies of dispatches from chargé d'affaires Spencer Eddy and other representatives in Russia. Mobs were said to be like packs of starving wolves, their frenzy placing foreigners as well as Jews in mortal peril. *Chicago News* correspondent Stanley Washburn, along with his Negro servant, sprinted into the Odessa consulate only yards ahead of pursuers. Other Americans were saved in the nick of time by Cossacks. Afterwards they described their thrill at hearing clattering hoofbeats on cobblestones and seeing sabers flash in the sun as troublemakers were routed. In Rostov, the sixteen-year-old daughter of a Chicago salesman was carried on horseback to the consulate. "My Cossack captain was very romantic," she said. "He looked exactly like Pawnee Bill, and I shall love him forever." Mobs stoned United States consulates in Riga, Rostov, and Odessa. Squadrons of cavalry had to guard the buildings during two months of pogrom and revolutionary crisis.[19]

Albert Leffingwell, consul at Warsaw and former president of the American Humane Society, took in so many refugees that he ran out of funds. There was no food, coal, or medical supplies. Americans under his roof were suffering terribly, he said in a cable asking the State Department to wire money immediately. In addition, he wanted to do something for Warsaw's Jews. Many had been murdered (he had seen Cossacks shooting them in a square near the consulate), and thousands were wounded and homeless. "Now is the time when America should send bread to the starving women and children of this land, without making inquiry into their religion or race," he wrote. In the opinion of Secretary Root,

Leffingwell had been unwise in extending himself beyond his means. All requests were turned down, including one that he be recompensed for money spent out of his own pocket. Describing himself as ill, exhausted, and unable to face the prospect of a winter without heat, Leffingwell departed for the Italian Riviera, where he rejected all of Root's demands that he return to his post.[20]

Consul C. A. Heenan, in Odessa, felt differently about the pogroms—the conduct of Jews had been arrogant in the extreme; they had manufactured bombs in their homes and had threatened to throw sulfuric acid in the face of anyone who attacked them. "In my opinion they have been very imprudent," he said. Chargé Eddy immediately relayed this information to Washington: "The reports from Mr. Heenan indicate that the Jews have taken a leading part in all disturbances and that the attack upon them would not have occurred if they had remained quietly in their homes."[21]

Eddy met the train from Berlin on December 8. During the ride back to the embassy, he asked Meyer for an extended leave of absence in the United States. The past two months had been nerve-racking, and Eddy had averaged only four hours of sleep each night. The ambassador understood perfectly, telling Eddy that he would not be needed during the more restful weeks that lay ahead. Russia had seen the last of her troubles, Meyer said. He had heard just an hour before, from a Russian official on the train, that the government was prepared to mobilize another four hundred and fifty thousand Cossacks. With pride he recalled the roles played by himself and Roosevelt in freeing troops for use against the revolution. He was certain that Americans in Russia would receive adequate protection in the future.[22]

Roosevelt, in the meantime, had been undergoing a different kind of siege. He could go nowhere in Washington without being confronted by foreign-looking individuals, often with unkempt beards and wrinkled suits, who called out for him to do something about Russia's Jews. An actress from

New York, a Miss Dorée, had approached Mrs. Roosevelt on the steps of the Episcopal Church and made remarks so imprudent that she had been arrested. Jewish petitioners from all over the country had come to the White House. Standing at an office window, the president could watch the procession, read the placards, and hear cheers and applause from groups of people surrounding gesticulating orators. Some speakers, he heard, were calling for a general strike of Jewish workers throughout the nation.[23]

Of the hundreds of letters and telegrams arriving daily, those from influential sources found their way to the president's desk. Joseph Barondess pointedly recalled that the United States government had sent a note of protest to the Tsar at the time of the Kishinev pogrom in 1903. The Hebrew Veterans of the War with Spain asked Roosevelt to remember that humanitarian spirit which once had moved him up San Juan Hill in the name of Cuban freedom. "Exert your wonderful influence," urged New York's Board of Aldermen. Simon Wolf, speaking for B'nai B'rith, congratulated Roosevelt on his enormous prestige and suggested that he apply it once again. Most numerous and annoying were telegrams from Jacob Schiff. His proposals, which included sending the Navy to the mouth of the Neva, irritated the president by their extravagance and by their tone. While others begged, Schiff demanded. While others flattered, Schiff implied that American policy lacked virility, a national characteristic of which Roosevelt was most proud.[24]

Pressure from the Jewish press came largely in the form of reminders that the president never before had been so careful about using personal influence in international affairs: Why should he hide the Big Stick now? Were his relations with Nicholas so fragile that they could not survive a moderately worded expression of disapproval? The Jewish press noted that a protest from the president need not be brusque, nor need it come under the heading of official policy. "A brief personal note from him will save lives," *Jewish Comment* said. "Will he write it?"[25]

The answer was no. According to historians Tyler Dennett and Philip C. Jessup, Roosevelt had protested the Kishinev pogrom for the purpose of winning Jewish votes in the election of 1904. No such problem faced him now. Moreover, the Kishinev matter had arisen at a time when American policy, because of Far Eastern concerns, had been openly hostile to the Russian government. This problem too had evaporated. Answering his mail, Roosevelt expressed sympathy but said there was absolutely nothing he could do. "We did not want to make Russia sensitive," he explained later. The *Nation* praised the decision, saying, "We should certainly resent it if Russia asked us to put a stop to lynchings."[26]

Among Jewish petitioners only Oscar Straus, former minister to Turkey, gained entry to the White House. The president repeated that he was powerless to do anything, but the New York mercantilist insisted upon knowing why. Awkward gaps appeared in the conversation. Roosevelt sent a message next door to the State Department, and Elihu Root arrived five minutes later. Upon regaining his breath (Straus assumed he had been running), the secretary launched an exposition of policy that lasted two hours.[27]

Root was opposed to diplomatic action in any form. He feared injury to Russian-American relations, and the possibility that protests would hurt Jews rather than help them. Root also felt that the Tsar could do nothing even if he wanted to because pogroms arose from deep-seated racial antagonisms that were complex and not easily dealt with. According to the reports Root was getting from his men in Russia, Jews themselves were not without blame for what had happened. Then too, Root wondered if the situation was truly that serious. Root had it on good authority, indeed from the Russian ambassador himself, that newspaper accounts of the pogroms had been grossly exaggerated. Rather than protest to the Tsar, he felt the American government might well consider a protest against those American Jews who were raising money to send to Russia. He feared that if part of this money should be used to buy weapons for the revolution, Nicholas would resent America, and rightly so. While nothing could be done about Russia, Root pointed out that it might be possible to protest against the treatment of Jews in Morocco. He asked Straus what he would think of that.[28]

Straus at last admitted that he could think of nothing the government could do about Russia. Root gave him two tickets to the Army-Navy football game, and Roosevelt later sent an appreciative letter saying, "Thank Heaven, you kept your head."[29]

The president drew a contrast between the reasonable and well-mannered Straus and the "hysterical" Jacob Schiff. He did not want to hurt Schiff's feelings—the reason he gave for not answering his November telegrams—but at last Roosevelt lost patience and informed the banker that he was making a fool of himself, damaging the good name of all American Jews, and making the United States government look ridiculous. Schiff had even gone so far as to cable the Russian government. In a sharp protest to Roosevelt, Witte charged that Schiff was meddling in Russian affairs. The president then wrote to Straus, asking what could be done to restrain "that other prominent Jewish gentleman" whose actions threatened serious harm to American-Russian relations. Roosevelt added that Schiff had already "prejudiced Witte against the cause for which he was pleading, by his attitude."[30]

Schiff and Straus were among thousands of Jews who were writing to their congressmen. Petitions, often with dozens of pages of signatures, arrived by parcel post from over twenty cities. Most wanted Congress to pass a joint resolution requesting action by the president. The Senate showed little interest, but a group of congressmen from New York City drafted a strong resolution for consideration by the House. It was announced on December 11 by Representative William Sulzer, who demanded that Roosevelt protest directly to the Tsar, for, as everyone knew, "the unspeakable brutalities . . . have been connived at by the Russian government and have been incited by the Russian ruling classes. . . . That must be stopped and stopped quickly. . . . Otherwise Russia, in the opinion of mankind, will and must stand indicted before the judgment bar of the world as beyond the pale of its civilization."[31]

The resolution went to the Committee on Foreign Affairs, where heated language dominated testimony both pro and con. A New York rabbi said that America had "forgotten its noblest traditions." A war veteran from Galveston, Texas, accused Jews of "expecting us to take up the cudgel for them whenever their arrogant, impudent, and insolent conduct brings the wrath of the non-Jewish population upon them." Secretary Root stressed his sympathy for pogrom victims, but informed the resolution's sponsors that they were wasting their time. Even if it passed, he said, it would have no effect upon American policy. "I cannot conceive," Root said, "that adoption would accomplish any good purpose." The committee also learned that Henry Cabot Lodge, guardian of the president's interests in the Senate, was opposed to the resolution and would never allow its joint expression.[32]

Some committee members wanted to pigeonhole the controversy, but news from Russia would not allow this. The pogroms continued into 1906, each slaughter bringing new loads of mail to offices in Washington. On June 22, 1906, Congress jointly resolved that "those bereaved have the hearty sympathy of the people of this country." Senator Lodge had given full approval, but Representative Sulzer disowned the feeble statement and stalked out of the House before the vote was taken.[33]

Gorky

8. A Triumph for Righteousness

THE POGROMS PROVED Witte's manifesto to be a fraud, just as St. Petersburg revolutionaries had suspected on the day of its proclamation. Yet the Soviet was repeatedly unsuccessful in its attempts to start another general strike. Workers in the capital remembered the perils and hardships of October and did not want to endure them again. Some distrusted the Soviet, which appeared to be increasingly interested in political, rather than union, goals. Miliukov clung desperately to his belief in the manifesto, looked forward to the constitution Witte was writing, and announced that liberals no longer could cooperate with parties that sought change through radical methods. General Trepov noted each new evidence of division among his enemies. At the same time government strength was growing. Much of the army had returned from the Far East, providing manpower for the new Cossack regiments Trepov organized in late November and early December. He employed some of these on the night of December 18.

Hoping to settle differences, some two hundred and thirty leaders of revolutionary groups had met at Soviet headquarters. Their debate was interrupted by shouts from outside the building, where there were three circles of troopers, the first rank converging stirrup to stirrup so that no one would be able to escape.

The mass arrest touched off a few disorganized walkouts in St. Petersburg. Trepov broke these easily, but he worried about reports of more serious insurrections elsewhere. Peasants were burning landlords' houses and placing themselves in control of extensive areas of the Caucasus, Poland, and the Baltic Provinces. There was fighting in Rostov, Kharkov, Novorossisk, and other cities. In Moscow, factory workers joined students in street demonstrations, destruction of trolley cars, and raids on municipal buildings. It was not a strike but civil war, the chief of police wired Trepov two hours before rebels killed him. In residential streets, crowds gathered at barricades of furniture, boxes, and dirty snow. Armed and uniformed soldiers—probably deserters from nonelite regiments, a police official said—taught factory men how to shoot and hugged the university girls who brought food and hot drinks. Warmed by tea, vodka, bonfires, and dancing, revolutionaries celebrated their apparent victory. From barricade to barricade traveled rumors that Trepov was dead or that the Tsar had fled the country. Christmas Eve brought rising temperatures and a blizzard. There were snowball raids between rival barricades, as well as cacophonous efforts to drown out one another's carols and revolutionary anthems.[1]

Ambassador Meyer was depressed by news from Moscow. He advised Root that Russia had gone insane; that the government was helpless, and only the revolutionists appeared to be well-organized. The Romanov dynasty might fall at any hour, Meyer said, giving way to socialists, communists, power-mad labor leaders, and only God knew what. There was one bright spot for Meyer—St. Petersburg remained safe and quiet. While attending the ballet, he found it "hard to believe that elsewhere a revolution was going on." When Trepov appeared at Princess Olga Orlov's dinner, Meyer congratulated him on how efficiently he had maintained order in the capital. Equally comforting to Meyer was the presence of a German fleet in the vicinity of Kronstadt, standing by to carry off the Tsar and other refugees if worst came to worst.[2]

Meyer's concerns included Americans in other parts of Russia. The most important businessmen had departed, but there were still a few life insurance salesmen stranded in far-off provinces. Receiving their desperate messages, Meyer made arrangements for transporting them back to the capital. The most urgent call came from the New York Air Brake Company at Lubertzy, a factory suburb of Moscow. Thomas C. Purdy, manager, was under siege in the machine shop. Strikers had made it clear that they would not allow him to leave until he had agreed to higher wage rates. As Purdy later admitted to Meyer, the wages he paid were very low. "Several families live in one room in squalor," he said. Yet—and Meyer tended to agree with him here—the workers themselves were to blame for these conditions. Purdy said that they had "no ambition to increase their earning power— they have the opportunity as it is piece work." Purdy found demands for libraries and latrines in the factory even more objectionable than the wage issue. Purdy vowed that he would never submit to these "social demands," even though his life was in danger. The threat of violence grew daily, he related in telegrams which he somehow managed to send to the embassy. Help arrived at last. In a grateful letter to Meyer, Purdy reported that Cossacks had restored order and broken the strike. Also at the ambassador's request, Cossacks ended a strike at the International Harvester Company in Omsk.[3]

By the end of December, Meyer could write, "The situation is improving in Moscow, and the revolutionists probably will fail." Reports from the Caucasus and Baltic Provinces were also reassuring. N. P. Bornholdt, United States consul in Riga, told Meyer that the effects of peace with Japan were now proving to be decisive. "Fortunately, the great reinforcement of the troops and the systematic plan pursued during the last weeks for the repression of the disturbance . . . has got the better of the revolution also in this part of Russia," Bornholdt said.[4]

The plan to which Bornholdt referred was calculated to put an end to revolutionary ideas once and for all. In the Baltic Provinces alone, over three thousand persons were executed by shooting, bayoneting, and hanging. Women were stripped, flogged with clubs, and left to freeze in the subzero temperatures. Not wishing to kill all prisoners, Cossacks broke legs and severed tendons as methods of handicapping individuals judged likely to cause trouble in the future. The story was much the same in Kharkov, Rostov, Poland, and the Caucasus. Prisoners sometimes were herded into theaters and other large buildings. After artillery fire destroyed the structures, soldiers machine-gunned survivors. Even in towns where no disturbances had taken place, police shot newspaper editors, librarians, and teachers suspected of spreading antigovernment opinions. In a few cases involving blatantly unpatriotic teachers, it was deemed necessary to execute their infected pupils as well. Prisons were packed, as were the long lines of cattle cars in trains bound for Siberia.[5]

Moscow's celebrating workers and students had neglected to capture the railway stations. On Christmas Day the Semenovsky Guards rolled in from St. Petersburg, along with Cossack regiments and units of light artillery. Five thousand rebels died as field guns smashed barricade after barricade, opening the streets for cavalry charges. The last resistance was crushed on December 30. Seventeen large buildings were designated as prisons—but only temporarily, since government officials for once unanimously favored liquidation of the revolutionaries. Nicholas was wryly amused by the attitude of Premier Witte: "Since the happenings in Moscow, he has radically changed his views; now he wants to hang and shoot everybody. I have never seen such a chameleon of a man."[6]

"Oh, why had we persuaded the Mikado to take his hands from the throat of the Tsar?" wondered a *New York Times* correspondent, sickened by frightful punishments and the renewed confidence with which the government administered them. The *Chicago Tribune* was more representative of current American opinion when it thanked God that the Semenovsky Guards had arrived in time. The *St. Paul Pioneer Press* protested against revolutionary activities during the Christmas season and noted that perpetrators had got what they deserved. Russians had received the gift of the manifesto with rude ingratitude, said the *Seattle Daily Times,* proving (in the view of various papers) that they were louts, fanatical unionists, crazy animals, maddened brutes, purveyors of hatred, and illiterate destroyers of all that was decent. The *Outlook* cited raving intellectuals as having been responsible for the Moscow uprising. Holding the same opinion, the *Atlanta Journal* advised Russian students to join in wholesome activities, such as football and fraternity life. A number of papers criticized Nicholas for being too lenient. He had let too many of them get away. After all, said the *Chicago News*, it was easy enough to spot a revolutionary in a crowd: "The moment you set eyes upon him you know. . . . His hair stands on end, his eyes are wild, and his dress is in disorder."[7]

Yelling "Hurrah for the Tsar" and "Keep America Free," crowds surrounded socialist meeting places in several cities. New York provided successful police protection, but in Chicago and Philadelphia uniformed officers joined the attacks.[8]

The outlook was anything but promising for revolutionaries preparing for personal appearance tours of the United

States. Gentleman socialist William E. Walling had assembled an elite corps of Russians who, because of famous names or acts of heroism, would be objects of admiration across the Atlantic. Holding classes in St. Petersburg cafés, Walling coached these men on their English and quizzed them on American sports, songs, and customs. He checked their table manners and advised on shaving beards and clipping mustaches. Upon arriving in New York, the Russians were told to accept the counsel of Ernest Poole as they shopped for suits, ties, hats, and accessories. Only Maxim Gorky objected to preparations which he found trivial and demeaning. He preferred to present himself to the American public as an honest man of the soil, brandishing unmanicured nails and daring any banker or merchant to criticize his peasant blouse and boots. Walling did not argue. Gorky could wear anything he pleased and still be the top attraction, his drawing power worth that of all the others combined. Together they would raise millions of dollars, a subject Walling mentioned too often. His knowledge of American customs and attitudes somehow did not take into account the change in mood that had occurred since his departure some six months before.[9]

Following a New York shopping tour and some last-minute advice from Poole, Moysey Gourevich presented himself as student hero of the Moscow barricades, and Gregory Maxim as leader of the abortive rebellion in the Baltic Provinces. An escape from Siberia hidden in a barrel of sauerkraut was Gregory Gershuni's claim to fame. The three *Bundists* had to cancel their tours after three or four appearances in nearly empty theaters. Maxim narrowly missed being captured by Philadelphia police, and two weeks later Gourevich fled from pursuers in the same city. It was disheartening, Gourevich said, that he should have to repeat his Russian escapades in the land of his benefactors. Henceforth they appeared only before socialist audiences, where prorevolutionary enthusiasm remained high and purses nearly empty. They took a few hundred dollars back to Russia, as well as a strong dislike for Walling. Before sailing, Maxim expressed random disillusionments: "America is the kingdom of capitalism. Here the dollar rules over everybody and everything. . . . There is no literature, no art, no press in America. A taste for the artistic is entirely unknown." Gershuni resented having had to relate, over and over again, the tale of his escape in the sauerkraut. Russian visitors were deadly serious about their fund-raising tours and disliked calling attention to the more spectacular, and even frivolous, events of their revolutionary careers.[10]

Touring liberals were even less successful, probably because, in emphasizing their distaste for Russian radicalism, they alienated the only Americans still interested in the revolution. Ivan Okuntsov was advertised as a deserter from the Cossacks, possessing the inside story of that infamous organization, and Alexis Alyadin was the Doomed Man of Russia, facing forty-five death sentences when he returned home. Sholem Aleichem, the famed literary figure, had survived the Kiev pogrom. Ivan Narodny appeared as Russia's Nathan Hale—a Miliukov spy who had worked as a clerk in the Ministry of Interior, been captured, and escaped from a dungeon in the Fortress of Peter and Paul.[11]

Collections were so small that new suits looked seedy from lack of pressing and railroad fares became a serious problem. Following their ejection from a train in central Illinois, Alyadin and Okuntsov slept in cornfields until Poole wired money. Narodny persevered for some weeks after the others had given up. Speaking mainly to Jewish audiences, he raised enough money to buy some hand grenades. Poole described how Narodny departed one night, staggering under boxes marked with soap labels, and was "never heard from again."[12]

Much had been expected of Nicholas Tchaikovsky, largely because of the fame of his older brother Peter Ilitch. After several weeks of a disappointing money-raising tour—due in some part to his inability to grant requests that he play the piano—the Social Revolutionary called upon Mark Twain for advice. Twain described his guest as grizzled, tired, and depressed. Tchaikovsky told Twain that he could not understand how Americans could be so indifferent when only four months before, in November, they had given over a million dollars for pogrom relief. "I was forced to clarify the picture for him and give it to him straight," Twain later wrote. He told Tchaikovsky that the million dollars had come from Jews. "Our Christianity is a sham, and we have lost our ancient sympathy with oppressed peoples struggling for life and liberty," he said. To support this view, the novelist recalled events of the previous summer, when Theodore Roosevelt had delivered a death blow to the revolution. He cursed the president flamboyantly but ended on a hopeful note. "Some of us," he said, ". . . may live to see the blessed day when Tsars and Grand Dukes are as scarce as I trust they are in Heaven." When Tchaikovsky returned to Russia, police penetrated his disguise and locked him in the Fortress of Peter and Paul as punishment for his activities in America.[13]

A year before, at about the time of Bloody Sunday, a book version of Maxim Gorky's play, *The Lower Depths*, as well as two of his novels, had been on American best-seller lists. Advertising *The Peasant* as suppressed in Russia, the *New York Herald* had run the novel in daily installments. Delivery wagon posters had announced the appearance of Gorky short stories in magazines, and a poem, "The Stormy Petrel," had been reprinted in papers throughout the country. These were brooding, brutal works, critics had said, but their shock value was highly important to the great task of stirring up opposition to Tsarist tyranny. Americans had also grown familiar with exciting episodes from Gorky's own life. Magazine writers had described a young man who worked as a shoemaker, cook on a Volga River steamer, baker, choirboy, icon painter, and fruit seller, all the while reading books and trying to improve his mind. Success had come, only to be snatched away and rewarded by imprisonment and torture. A *Collier's* version had told of the woman Gorky loved, the charming and beautiful actress Maria Andreyeva, who read his letters over and over again during the lonely days and nights of waiting in the small apartment she had rented near the Fortress of Peter and Paul. *Everybody's* called it the tearful and heart-rending story of two people who symbolized the agony of all Russians. Americans had been moved to demand the prisoner's release in articles, editorials, and petitions to the Tsar. At first these efforts had been detrimental to Gorky's treatment, but he had been free for several weeks when Walling and Bullard approached him in November 1905.[14]

The writer was not keen on their plan to send him to America, no matter how often they described his fantastic popularity there. First to give in was Maria Andreyeva, who thought it would be a pity to pass up the millions of dollars that could be made for the revolution. Gorky at last agreed, provided that he could wear his own clothes and take Andreyeva with him. She did not object, nor did Walling, who judged that an attractive actress would prove an asset to the tour.[15]

Tutoring sessions were interrupted when Gorky went to Moscow and spent Christmas in the barricades. Once again the object of a manhunt, he reappeared in St. Petersburg only long enough to allow Andreyeva to pack and to inform Walling that the American tour must begin immediately. The fugitives escaped over the Finnish border. After somewhat leisurely travels through Germany, Switzerland, and France, they sailed for America in early April.

Failure of police to capture Gorky before he left the country worried Premier Witte and officials in the Foreign Ministry. The mission had already received considerable attention in European and American newspapers. Revolutionaries of lesser fame were being ignored in the United States, but it was difficult to imagine a similar response to Maxim Gorky.

The inconstant nature of democratic press opinion, although a comfort to Nicholas in recent months, required a watchful eye. If Gorky himself could no longer be halted, it might be possible to destroy his mission.

In Washington, Ambassador Rosen received his instructions. He placed the matter in the hands of Colonel E. Nicolaev, the embassy's chief of intelligence. Nicolaev had no trouble finding a family portrait of Gorky with his wife, Katherine Pavlovna, and their five- and eight-year-old sons. Copies were mailed to all New York newspapers, along with accounts of how the writer had deserted his family, had not bothered to obtain a divorce, and would now insult Americans by flaunting his mistress in their presence.

A spy in the embassy sent details of the plot to Gorky's American sponsors—Leroy Scott, Poole, Cahan, Wilshire, and Hilquit. "This is dynamite," Poole said. All agreed that Gorky must be warned while still aboard ship, so that he could find a hiding place for Andreyeva before reporters reached him. Later the woman could be spirited off the ship and taken to some secret place where she could remain for the duration of the visit. Thus Nicolaev's story could be denied.

On the morning of April 10, the *Kaiser Wilhelm der Grosse* reached the quarantine station in New York harbor. Scott, Poole, and the others rode a revenue cutter to the liner. Hurrying along the *Wilhelm*'s decks, they looked ahead and saw that they were too late. Both Russians stood by the rail. Powder flashes from cameras had startled Andreyeva, and Gorky was patting her hand reassuringly as he tried to comprehend the questions of nearly two dozen reporters. His interpreter arrived with Scott's party, allowing the interview to begin.

How did Gorky like America? reporters asked. It was a marvelous country, he replied. He said that he had always dreamed of coming to the United States because "things are so bright and lovely here, and people can pursue their happiness freely." What about the Statue of Liberty? he was asked. One newsman noted that the Russian's eyes grew moist as he regarded the "giant limbs" of the statue. And what of the skyscrapers? was another question. From what Gorky could see as he leaned over the rail, he liked them very much. "They are lovely, gigantic," he said. "They seem to kiss the clouds."

Reporters scribbled happily. Because they appeared to approve of Gorky and his companion, Scott dared ask the question he had in mind: Would they consider repressing the story their papers had received from Colonel Nicolaev? Agreement was unanimous. The relieved Scott was told that New York's editors already had decided not to print what they considered to be a particularly vile attempt by the Russian government to create a scandal.

On the piers at Hoboken a crowd of thousands—not all from the East Side, papers noted later—pressed forward to welcome the visitors. Those who fell into the water were rescued. A band played Sousa's "Hands Across the Sea" as young men hoisted Gorky on their shoulders and bore him to a Hudson River ferry. He was "half paralyzed with delight and wonder," the *Sun* reported, at the cheers and applause he drew along the length of Broadway.[16] In the Belleclaire Hotel, at Broadway and Seventy-seventh Street, the Russians received a royal welcome from the manager, Milton Roblee. Mr. and Mrs. Gorky were his most famous guests ever, and he would be eternally grateful, he said, if they would mention to the Associated Press that they were stopping at the Belleclaire.

The evening papers carried front-page pictures and stories that portrayed the pair in flattering terms—a slender, shy, and pretty woman who gazed worshipfully at her husband, a dashing, romantic figure with suffering eyes, drooping black mustache, and peasant blouse and boots. That night, after returning from a banquet in his honor, Gorky stared in fascination from his ninth-story window. He said that he never had seen anything so beautiful as the millions of lights. "From the depths of dark city blocks, buildings of twenty-eight, of thirty-three stories rise skyward. It is all stupendous." He burst into tears, telling sponsors that he could not find the words to express enough gratitude for the warmth of his reception.

Mark Twain, who was arranging a banquet to be attended by America's leading authors, was pleased by what appeared to be a resurgence of interest in the Russian revolution. Yet he was too cynical to believe that it was anything other than a temporary phenomenon, produced by Gorky's standing as a celebrity. A friend, novelist William Dean Howells, agreed that the press was fickle, would soon grow bored, and in the end the revolutionist would be lucky to raise several thousand dollars.

Excitement grew steadily during the first week of the visit. A report that the Russians had been asked to the White House was quickly denied by Roosevelt, but there were other invitations. In the beginning Gorky appeared mainly at socialist gatherings, but these were often attended by such literary lights as Twain, Howells, Ida Tarbell, Bliss Carman, David Graham Phillips, Finley Peter Dunne, S. S. McClure, Edwin Markham, Charles A. Beard, and the touring English novelist H. G. Wells. John Mitchell, president of the United Mine Workers, and a good friend of Roosevelt's, asked Gorky for an appointment, and the next day a leading real estate broker showed the Russian couple around the city in his automobile. Invitations began to arrive from the business luncheon clubs. Newspapers noted Gorky's presence at a function in the St. Regis Hotel and announced that he soon would make a speech in Carnegie Hall. And shortly he would go on display in the drawing rooms of lower Fifth Avenue. The first invitations from social leaders arrived at the Belleclaire on the day after newspapers revealed that Lady Warwick, an English countess, had sold her jewels to raise money for Gorky's cause. The Friends of Russian Freedom, dominated by persons of wealth and social prominence, had been dormant for several months, but now it regrouped committees and reestablished communications with chapters in other parts of the country. Philadelphia announced a schedule that promised to occupy Gorky's every hour in that city. Chicago's Opera House was made available, and Alice Stone Blackwell was pleased to announce that hallowed Faneuil Hall would be the site of Boston's homage. Twain was astonished. Much was happening that reminded him of the period following Bloody Sunday. He began to think that he had been too pessimistic, that Gorky might in truth be able to rekindle the spirit of the previous year.

The pace was so furious, sometimes seven or eight entertainments in a single day, that the guest of honor "could not think straight." During a reception in the Belleclaire on April 13, a Friday, one of his sponsors asked a question. Gaylord Wilshire wanted to know if Gorky would like to send a telegram of hope and encouragement to two oppressed people who had been thrown into jail because of their socialist beliefs. (Wilshire failed to mention that the two people, Bill Haywood and Charles Moyer, had been charged with the murder of Frank Steunenberg, former governor of Idaho.) Gorky, preoccupied with a group of admirers, nodded yes. Wilshire, who already had written the telegram, signed Gorky's name and released a copy to the press. It read: "Greetings to you, my brother socialists. Courage! The day of justice and deliverance for the oppressed of all the world is at hand." Some papers ignored the story, but the *Sun,* *Herald,* and *Times* were highly critical of a foreigner who repaid America's hospitality by condoning assassination and inciting revolution. Gorky called a press conference and tried to explain that he had not understood the facts of the case. He disowned the telegram and said that he was angry with Wilshire for having tricked him. He said that he admired the democratic American system and had no wish to see it altered.[17]

It is possible that Gorky's popularity could have survived a single blunder, but he had made others. The decision to bring Andreyeva with him had been anything but wise, and the truth about her remained a secret only so long as he was able to charm all of the newspapermen in New York City.

This was impossible, as he learned at the disastrous Belleclaire reception. Within an hour after Wilshire had posed his question, Gorky was asked another. An editor of the *New York World* wanted to know if he would write a series of exclusive articles about his revolutionary adventures. Gorky declined, explaining that he already had signed a contract with Mr. Hearst's *Evening Journal.* Knowing nothing of America's most bitter press feud, the Russian was surprised when the editor muttered an obscenity and departed without another word.

The next morning *World* newsboys flaunted papers with enormous headlines: "GORKY BRINGS ACTRESS HERE AS 'MME GORKY'." Beneath, side by side, were pictures of Andreyeva and the deserted wife, along with an account of the writer's private life based upon information supplied by Colonel Nicolaev. The same story and pictures, but with heavier stress on the moral issue, appeared a few hours later in an extra edition of the *Herald*. Apparently the two exposures were disconnected in motive. Poole attributed the *Herald*'s reversal of policy to pressures applied by the publisher's current mistress, an extremely patriotic Russian countess.

World in hand, manager Milton Roblee informed Gorky that he was no longer welcome at the Belleclaire. "My hotel is a family hotel," he said, mentioning that several other guests had threatened to check out. Wilshire arrived while the Russians were packing. He tried to persuade Roblee to change his mind. "Look here, old man," he said, "if you will only let this great man stay here, your hotel will be famous."[18]

"I've had too much advertising from him already," the manager replied.

"The Waldorf would take him in a minute," Wilshire argued.

"Bet a hundred they wouldn't."

"Just give them until tomorrow morning."

"I'll give them just long enough to pack their traps and get out, no longer," was the manager's final word.

Gorky, laden with suitcases, appeared in the lobby. The *Press* said that he was crying again, but the *Brooklyn Eagle* described his mood as coldly belligerent as he rejected all of Wilshire's attempts to help carry the suitcases, pay the hotel bill himself, and arrange for the couple to stay in his own home. According to the *Herald,* Gorky was brazenly calm and self-assured in defending his moral attitudes: "It is in the great and tragic moments of life that I find the real Maxim Gorky. I am always strongest when I stand alone. The bitter cup contains the noblest wine of life, and I am not afraid to drain it. All is harmony in my soul. There is music in the air and an atmosphere of poetry all about. . . . This woman is my wife in every sense. I love her and she loves me. . . . She and I both consider it beneath us to go into any explanation."

It was late afternoon before Gorky, with the help of Leroy Scott, found a hotel proprietor who would provide rooms. Antoine Lablanche, at the Lafayette-Brevoort on lower Fifth Avenue, gave assurances that it was not his custom to inquire into the private business of guests. Lablanche changed his mind within the hour. The Russians had unpacked, but had hardly sampled the complimentary fruit, before they were evicted. The bill for $12.40 included the fruit.

Using false names, Gorky and Andreyeva registered at the Rhinelander, across the street from the Lafayette-Brevoort. There was no time to rest—indeed no time to bathe and change clothes—for a dinner-dance in their honor had already begun at the Grand Central Palace. Gorky was certain that the affair had been canceled, or that no one would attend, as he told Scott during the drive to the Palace.

He was surprised, and at first pleased, by the clamor that greeted his entrance to the ballroom. Women ogled and squealed, but most refused to speak to the notorious pair. Some stood on chairs to get a better look, only to be knocked to the floor where they sat crying while they rubbed ankles or knees. One woman's gown was "ripped in a manner that caused her to be taken immediately from the hall." Then, as the *Times* put it, "order was restored, the broken chairs were removed, and dancing begun."[19] In Scott's carriage on the way back to the hotel, Gorky was tired and depressed. He said that he felt like the man with three arms, an unfortunate creature he had pitied three days earlier at Barnum and Bailey's Circus.

They reached the Rhinelander a little after midnight. It was raining heavily. Scott watched his friends hurry across the sidewalk, Gorky sheltering his companion with a newspaper. When they disappeared behind the revolving doors, he told his driver to go on.

The Gorky luggage was stacked in the lobby. "You will have to go," said Frank Derity, propietor. The interpreter having left with Scott, Gorky could only curse in Russian and wave his hands wildly. As the *Eagle* explained: "He was a little bit tired of this continuous performance of ejectment from hotels. He wanted to stay until . . . morning, but Mr. Derity was obdurate."[20]

After watching the "soaking-wet revolutionaries" try at the Victoria and other hotels, journalists either lost the trail or lost interest, for further bulletins were vague and conflicting. One placed the couple at Grand Central Station, waiting for the 5:10 train to Montreal. Another reported an embarkation aboard the Staten Island Ferry.

English writer H. G. Wells was deeply concerned about the couple. In the days that followed he searched everywhere but could find no trace of the Russians. He feared that they had met with violence. "On one day Gorky was at the zenith," Wells wrote later in *The Future of America*. "On the next he had been swept from the world. . . . It was terrifying." A week passed before Wells discovered the couple in a Staten Island cottage owned by English socialists John and Prestonia Martin. Gorky seemed relaxed and happy. He was helping Prestonia write a book on the nonadvancement of civilization since the Age of Pericles. There was wine, good conversation, and songs around bonfires on the beach. Wells was glad, for Gorky's sake, that the Martins did not subscribe to any newspapers.

Under the heading "Latest Insult to American Decency," the *Pittsburgh Sun* editorialized: "Do you respect the virtue of your mother? Do you prize the chastity of your wife? Forty million men live in these United States and every one of them will answer 'Yes' to these questions. And what is more, every man will mean what he says. . . . Upon the American Home depends the future of the American Nation. . . . Today the country is aroused because of the insult that has been offered to the purity of its women, to the sanctity of its homes, by Maxim Gorky, the novelist and agitator."21

Throughout the country the phrases varied but slightly. The Russians were said to be living in sin, advertising adultery, vulgar in appearance, warped in mind, stained of soul, defilers of marriage vows, corruptors of the home, and contaminators of family life. "That horrible creature Maxim Gorky," Senator Knute Nelson of Minnesota told the Associated Press, "is about as immoral as a man can be."22

The *Presbyterian* polished off "Socialism and Sensuality" in a single editorial. Bishop McFaul told a meeting of Catholic Charities that socialism and divorce worked hand in hand, one destroying property and the other the home. "Look at Maxim Gorky, the Russian socialist, coming to America to ask us to turn upon Russia," the bishop said. "That villain and scoundrel and polluter of womanhood would preach to us the gospel of human liberty." The *New York Sun* concluded that to win the support of Americans, a foreign revolution must "clothe itself in immaculate and conventional respectability and observe rigidly the tenets of morality."[23]

Columnist Burton Beach wrote in the *New York Commercial Advertiser:* "The whole affair of Gorkyism went smash, as if an American Vesuvius had blown its head off on Manhattan Island. There was fire, smoke, and ashes and lava everywhere, and a universal scattering for shelter."[24] Society women canceled all invitations. Labor leader John Mitchell made certain that the press knew of his decision not to meet with Gorky. Howells and Twain withdrew their support. "His blunder was worse than a crime," Howells fumed. "Poor fellow," Twain said, "he didn't understand our bigotry. . . . Too bad." The "social lynching" was ridiculous, of course, but Twain was a realist. Gorky's mistake had ruined his effectiveness, and Twain felt that further efforts in his behalf would be wasted. In canceling the authors' dinner he had arranged, Twain explained: "Custom is custom; it is built of brass, boiler iron, granite; facts, reasonings, arguments have no more effect upon it than the idle winds have upon Gibraltar. . . . There can be but one wise thing for a visiting stranger to do—find out what the country's customs are and refrain from offending against them."

Gorky's sponsors received cancellation notices from Philadelphia, Cincinnati, St. Louis, and every other city where appearances had been scheduled. Alice Stone Blackwell, shaken by the "horrid news," sent word that Faneuil Hall no longer was available. To be on the safe side, Boston's mayor announced that Gorky would not be permitted to enter the city. A New York paper said: "Chicago women of social prominence are almost a unit in declaring that Gorky and his companion must be repulsed. Local socialists will receive Gorky and the actress with cordiality." On this last point the reporter had failed to check with Chicago socialists, most of whom believed that to welcome the Russians might be interpreted as showing a preference for "European standards of moral ethics."[25]

United States Commissioner of Immigration T. Watchorn

stated that he would not like to act on the basis of "mere rumor," but admitted that he was under heavy pressure to deport Andreyeva under section two of the immigration law of 1903, which stated that women could not be brought to the United States for immoral purposes. The threat of deportation convinced a number of New York editors that matters were being carried too far. Carefully qualified defenses of Gorky began to appear. To be sure, editors said, his personal moral standards were primitive and not to be admired, but they wondered if he deserved obliteration. Was this the land of Mrs. Grundy? journalists asked, who feared that Europeans might think so, for already embarrassing dispatches had arrived from abroad. Jokes about puritanical Americans were circulating in London, and Paris was up in arms over the treatment accorded a great artist. The *Commercial Advertiser* discussed poetic license and tolerance of bohemian standards. The *World*, which had started the trouble, compiled a list of famous persons who had been forgiven "certain bad actions similar to those of Gorky"— Adam and Eve had not been married; only last year opera tenor Enrico Caruso had pinched several women near the monkey house in Central Park; and what of Voltaire, Admiral Nelson, Lord Byron, George Sand, and the great Irish nationalist Parnell?[26]

When Gorky heard about the great controversy he called a news conference at his Staten Island retreat. It was repugnant, he said, to be forced to discuss details of his private life, but he was willing to do so for the sake of the cause in Russia. He had been divorced from Katherine Pavlovna and married to Andreyeva under civil law administered by the Provisional Government of the Baltic States, a revolutionary body that had ceased to exist after Cossack operations of the previous December. Previously he had applied to the Church for a divorce, he said, but had been turned down because of his political views. He had cabled his former wife, asking her to confirm his story, and now showed reporters her recently delivered reply. Pavlovna said that she had remarried, was living comfortably in Yalta, and that Gorky's explanation was correct in every detail. She added that she was "very indignant at the intrusion into the personal and intimate life of a man, and astonished that the Americans, citizens of a free country, [were] not free from the prejudices dead already even with us in Russia."[27]

"No dice," said James Keeley, managing editor of the *Chicago Tribune*, when Jane Addams asked him to print the latest version of the story; most editors must have made similar decisions.[28] Only three New York papers published the Pavlovna message, but these apparently were enough to convince Gorky that his reputation had been salvaged. It was also true that his Carnegie Hall address had not yet been canceled. Therefore, in late April he prepared for his second entrance into New York City.

No one came to the Battery to meet his ferry, and in the evening he looked out on a deserted Carnegie Hall. With Andreyeva he attended a reception in the apartment of Professor John Dewey, the progressive educator who had wanted his Barnard College students to meet the celebrated couple. Learning of this "social atrocity," the *Chicago Inter-Ocean* charged Dewey with having "extremely peculiar, and even un-American, social and moral ideas. . . . It may well be wondered whether Barnard is a desirable institution for young ladies." Similar assertions in other papers forced the college to promise that Dewey would be investigated. A Barnard dean defended the students who had attended the reception: "I feel certain it was because they did not know the identity of the woman. You see, few of our girls read the daily papers."[29]

In the weeks that followed, Gorky visited several cities and spoke to those socialist organizations that would have him. The financial return paid his expenses, but no more. Meanwhile he was preparing his revenge—an article entitled "The City of Mammon: My Impressions of America," which was published in the August 1906 number of *Appleton's Magazine*. He recalled his hopes when he had first seen the Statue of Liberty, "not noticing on that glorious day the green rust on the dark bronze. . . . I did not know . . . that the passionate idealism of the young democracy had also become covered with rust." Skyscrapers no longer enchanted him. "These dull, heavy piles rise up into the sky, stern, cheerless, and morose . . . like black, uneven teeth. . . . In great houses dwell small people," he said. In Gorky's view, Americans were smug, round, lardy creatures, and also depraved, cruel, greedy, and uncultured. Even so, he wrote, it might be possible for foreigners to respect them if they were not such pious hypocrites. "I am willing to think that Americans are the best moralists in the world," he commented, asserting that all talk of their missions, crusades, and responsibilities for freedom abroad "was quite beyond the power of my nostrils to endure."

The article instigated twelve hundred letters of protest, most telling Gorky and Andreyeva to go back to Russia. This they could not do. Their destination was the Isle of Capri, where Gorky hoped to rest in the sun and cure the slight case of tuberculosis he had contracted in America.

He would recall some twenty years later that Americans had rejected him mainly because of his politics. When he had first arrived in the United States, the feelings of most people—fear of radicalism and revolution—had been obscured by their awe for his reputation as one of the world's great writers. Suddenly vulnerable because of the Andreyeva matter, he had experienced an attack all the more savage because of earlier restraints. Similar explanations had been offered by Mark Twain, Morris Hilquit, and others who had written on the subject.

Not until 1917, during an exhausting war that could not be ended in time to save him, would Nicholas II face insurrection so purposeful as that which he had crushed in December. The 1905 revolution was over, although no one could know this with certainty during the year that followed. To be on the safe side, Nicholas allowed an elected Duma to convene in early May. Having won 178 of the 524 seats, Miliukov's Constitutional Democratic party was the largest of the so-called opposition groups. William Jennings Bryan remained interested in Russia's prospects for democracy, and he went there to advise the Duma. He was disappointed time and again—by the firing of Premier Witte (the Tsar considered him too clever for his own good), by the Duma's impotence (the government allowed it to discuss nothing more important than the question of a new laundry for the University of Dorpat), by the arbitrary dissolution of the Duma in July (Miliukov's party had been impertinent in demanding an investigation of pogroms), and by the execution of over five hundred persons who had protested the dissolution. But Bryan was most disappointed because members of the Duma had not sought his advice. He thought some of the liberals had appeared to be positively hostile towards him.[30]

If Russians had been slow to understand America's response to their revolution, the Gorky affair allowed no further confusion. The government publicized it in full detail, and Ambassador Meyer was proud that his country was the subject of Russia's biggest news sensation since the end of the war with Japan. "It is quite remarkable," he said, "what interest the Russians take in Gorky having been turned down in America and how it pleases them." He was speaking of friends in the government, whom he saw often in view of rapidly expanding social opportunities. In reports to Washington, he ridiculed the Duma and spoke of deep affection for the United States among ministers and noblemen. Secretary Root urged Meyer to reciprocate all kindnesses and to keep reminding the regime that "there has been apparent in the United States a strong and rapidly-increasing friendly sympathy with Russia." Diplomatic relations were perfect,

Meyer believed, and he saw no reason why his summer vacation in western Europe could not begin two or perhaps three
weeks earlier than originally planned.[31]

Incensed by the Gorky episode, SDS and SRS no longer re-
frained from denouncing the United States for interfering in
the war, for remaining silent on the pogrom issue, and for
asking the Tsar to employ Cossacks as strikebreakers at
American-owned factories. The same criticisms someday
would find their way into works of Soviet history, which
often say that America revealed her opposition to Russian
socialism in 1905 rather than in the more commonly cited
intervention and nonrecognition decisions of 1918 to 1920. A
typical version (in *Krasnyi Arkhiv*) states that the United
States left no stone unturned in seeking means to support
the Tsarist throne, and that American diplomats were most
concerned about "the fate of foreign capital and enterprises
in Russia. In utterances filled with hatred for the struggle of
the Russian workers and peasants for freedom, they evalu-
ated the revolution mainly in terms of how it would threaten
. . . the established order in other lands. . . . The class instinct, however, warned these representatives that the victory
of Tsarism over the workers was only temporary and that the
Russian working class was beaten but not conquered."[32]

The revolution of 1905 was not necessarily a step along a
straight and narrow path leading to November 1917. Russian liberals in 1906 believed that *their* revolution was the
one that had been defeated. They were certain that a constitutional system would have been established and maintained following a collapse of the Tsar. They were equally
certain that the United States had done much to prevent that
collapse. Like the socialists, liberals resented Portsmouth, the
pogrom silence, and the Gorky rebuff. A group of twenty-five
writers demanded an apology from New York City, saying
that it had "offended Russian authors in the person of
Maxim Gorky and Russian womanhood in the person of
Madame Andreyeva by interfering with their private affairs."

Liberals were keenly aware that a nation that symbolized democracy had worked against their interests. Tragic irony, curious paradox, backstabbing, and hypocrisy—such were the terms employed by Vladimir Simkhovich, Leo Tolstoy, Paul Miliukov, and others in referring to the United States. "Could any Russian liberal have expected, even one year ago," the *Vilna Hasunan* asked in April 1906, "that the United States of America, among all the countries of the earth, would emerge as the greatest friend of the autocracy?"[33]

It is probable that few Americans cared what disappointed Russians were saying about them in the years immediately following 1905. Revolution was a loathsome word during this period, a word associated with violent means and alien ends. Continuing Tsarist practices—Cossack atrocities, incessant pogroms, and the defeat of all attempts to form a meaningful Duma—were no longer useful to analogy minded reformers. While editors continued to obtain sensational headlines out of Russia's never-ending misery, these mainly concerned assassinations of bureaucrats, acts of arson committed by peasant mobs, and urban thuggery traceable to workers carrying the inevitable red flags. A new theme, endlessly repeated, held that Russia had taught American progressivism a valuable lesson—that reforms must be undertaken gradually and with great care; and that reforms must be designed to improve the operation of an existing system rather than drastically alter that system.

A few editors could grow as angry as Russian revolutionaries in criticizing the 1905 policies of the United States. That they were a small minority is indicated by the nature of some of their comments. *Christian Advocate:* "Where Tsarist butchery is concerned . . . we all maintain a discreet silence. It is intolerable—it is monstrous." *Outlook:* "Why is it that Americans are . . . no longer against the Tsar?" *American Israelite:* "The press has totally ignored . . . the Bialystok pogrom." Wendell Phillips Stafford, quoted in

Menorah: "Is America heartless, or afraid to speak?" *Painter and Decorator:* "Have we become a nation of cowards? Is it not too late even now to keep the promise we made to the Russians." An unnamed Methodist clergyman, quoted in *American Israelite:* "We have failed, we have failed, and the oppressed of all the earth must forever more look elsewhere for encouragement in their strivings to be free."[34]

In the Progressive Era, when all things seemed possible to Americans, outraged critics concentrated their fire upon the nation's *failure to act* in behalf of Russian freedom. That failure was humiliating in its contrast to the easily recollected promises of early 1905 and before. From the sadder, and perhaps wiser, perspective of 1969, one looks back with the knowledge that all things are not possible, not even for the United States. Now it is possible to trace a long history of unfulfilled commitments. In the ninetenth century foreigners often inferred commitments from exuberant promises made by journalists and citizens' pressure groups. At critical moments the United States government was forced to disassociate its own policies from those of the public. In the twentieth century the government itself became an originator of impractical commitments, among them the Open Door policy, the Fourteen Points of Woodrow Wilson, the liberation policy of John Foster Dulles, and the war in Vietnam. Although he may resent this tradition, the modern "realist" need not admire all aspects of America's rejection of the 1905 revolution. While Roosevelt's intervention in the Russo-Japanese War was primarily dictated by long-range diplomatic concerns, responses to the pogroms and the Gorky tour were shaped more by bigotry and stupidity than by concepts of national interest.

In a general sense, however, the modern observer cannot be shocked, or outraged when he reads of America's failure to free Russia in 1905. He is mainly interested in that eternal first cause of diplomatic humiliation—the making of a promise rather than its breaking, that unfortunate chemistry of custom, principle, and moral intensity that produces an act of commitment at some point prior to reasonable consideration of its possibilities for fulfillment. At least one contemporary critic, Paul Miliukov, showed similar concerns.

In January 1908, Miliukov came to New York to address the Civic Forum. His speech was polite, even complimentary, but afterwards reporters extracted comments of a different sort.[35]

Russians despised the United States, Miliukov said in answer to the inevitable question. He made it clear that he could speak only for members of his own liberal party but believed that the feeling was shared by socialists as well.

Miliukov was asked why Russians did not like America and if it was because of the Gorky affair. He said that it was not; that the Gorky affair had been a silly thing, easily forgotten, except in the sense that it had been so perfectly symbolic of the larger, more important, rejection.

Was it the Portsmouth Treaty then; or the manner in which American holdings in Russia had been protected? reporters asked him. Not really, Miliukov implied. Nations could not be blamed for protecting their interests, he admitted; and in doing so, they often incurred fear or dislike— as in the case of British diplomacy—but never the kind of contempt Miliukov said Russians currently felt for the United States. Though he did not personally agree with it, he could respect the particular concept of interests that had led the United States government to oppose the revolution. He wished only that America's antirevolutionary policies had not followed "so much talk about love for freedom and morality." One could respect an enemy but never a hypocrite, he said. He proposed that one of two lessons must be learned if similar humiliations were to be avoided in the future: always be prepared to follow talk with action, or stop talking so much. The latter was the wiser choice, according to Miliukov.

A representative of the *New York Press* caught a flaw in Miliukov's reasoning: Had not the United States government been consistent in its opposition to the revolution? Had it made a single promise, even in the beginning? If Russians felt they had been misled, should not they place the blame on irresponsible newspapers, individuals, and private organizations?

Miliukov showed little desire to explore the intricacies of public opinion, except to admit that democracy, with its freedom of expression, was a formidable handicap to the operation of diplomacy. "This is your problem," he said. "Unfortunately it is not Russia's."

Newspapermen reported that Miliukov had grown warped and cynical since the time of his last visit to the United States in early 1905. On the day after his interview, however, he showed none of this cynicism, or even that he had been listening to his own comments on the folly of believing American promises.

He received a telegram from New York Congressman Herbert Parsons. Inviting the professor to come to Washington and meet the president, Parsons spoke of gala banquets and important conferences that were certain to be of benefit to Russia's struggle for freedom. Miliukov rushed to Pennsylvania Station and was in Washington some ten hours after having received his invitation.

Roosevelt refused to see him. In speculating upon the latest rebuff, some papers said that Congressman Parsons had been overly enthusiastic, failing to check with the White House before sending the invitation, apparently believing that the president would be agreeable once he heard that Miliukov had arrived in Washington. Others said that Roosevelt had approved the plan, then changed his mind. The *Independent* referred to "rumors that Russian ambassador Rosen [had] let it be known to the White House that his government frowned on the professor being received by Theodore Roosevelt." Other papers commented on the rapidity of Miliukov's return to New York and immediate departure for Europe: "He has been in this country only four days."[36]

Notes

1. The Challenge of Russia

1. Associated Press, June 2, 1903.
2. *Cincinnati Enquirer*, Dec. 10, 1903.
3. Salo W. Baron, *The Russian Jew Under Tsars and Soviets* (New York, 1964), pp. 52–70.
4. Bernard Pares, *The Fall of the Russian Monarchy* (New York, 1939), p.72.
5. Thomas A. Bailey, *A Diplomatic History of the American People* (New York, 1955), p. 58.
6. Norman A. Graebner, *Ideas and Diplomacy* (New York, 1964), pp. 88–9; Bailey, *Diplomatic History*, pp. 183–5; *Boston Recorder*, March 21, 1825.
7. *Register* and *Intelligencer* quoted in Elgin R. Coate, *American Trades Unions* (London, 1904), pp. 61, 64.
8. Bailey, *Diplomatic History*, p. 287.
9. Graebner, *Ideas and Diplomacy*, pp. 264–8; Bailey, *Diplomatic History*, pp. 210–11, 281–8; Merle Curti, "The Impact of the Revolution of 1848 on American Thought," *Proceedings of the American Philosophical Society* xciii (June 1949): 209–15.

10. Graebner, *Ideas and Diplomacy*, pp. 264–8; Bailey, *Diplomatic History*, pp. 210–11.
11. Ibid.
12. *New York Times*, March 24, 1871; *Chicago Tribune*, March 22, 1871; see also George L. Cherry, "American Metropolitan Press Reaction to the Paris Commune of 1871," *Mid-America* xxxii (Jan. 1950): 3–12.
13. Bailey, *Diplomatic History*, pp. 496–501.
14. *Commoner*, Feb. 10, 1905; *Florida Times-Union*, Nov. 26, 1904; "drunk" in *Christian Advocate*, May 6, 1905.
15. *Arena* (April 1905): 345, and (Jan. 1906): 78–80.
16. *Newark Daily Advertiser*, Nov. 26, 1906; farm problem in *California Cultivator*, April 16, 1905; "villified" in *Seattle Union Record*, Nov. 12, 1904.
17. Indians in *Commoner*, May 2, 1905; vigilantes in *International Quarterly* (July 1905): 274; *Independent*, Aug. 31, 1905; *Outlook*, Sept. 29, 1906; *Christian Advocate*, Aug. 3, 1905.
18. *Review of Reviews* (Dec. 1905): 643; *World Today* (March 1905): 233; Bryan in *Commoner*, Nov. 10, 1905.
19. Stanley K. Schultz, "The Morality of Politics: The Muckrackers' Vision of Democracy," *Journal of American History* (Dec. 1965): 527–47.
20. *Christian Evangelist*, June 12, 1904; *Bookman* (March 1905): 15.
21. *Christian Advocate*, June 20, 1904; *Jewish Exponent*, July 8, 1904; *Independent*, Aug. 15, 1904; *Christian Observer*, Oct. 20, 1904.
22. *Jewish Exponent*, Dec. 8, 1906; *American Israelite*, June 28, 1906; *Christian Advocate*, March 2, 1905; *Cincinnati Enquirer*, July 12, 1904.
23. *Hull House Bulletin* vii, no. 1 (1905–06): 20–23; *New York Herald*, May 28, 1905; information on dime novels from Mrs. Vladimir Woytinsky in an interview, Aug. 3, 1962, Washington, D.C.

2. Bloody Sunday

1. *Chicago News,* August 20, 1904.
2. *Sun, Press, Post, Transcript* and *Review of Reviews* quoted in *Literary Digest,* Aug. 6 and Sept. 3, 1904; *Times* referred to in *Providence Daily Journal,* July 30, 1904; *Independent,* Feb. 16, 1905; *Detroit News,* July 29, 1904; *North American Review* (Sept. 1904): 473–4; *Florida Times-Union,* July 31, 1904.
3. *American Israelite,* August 11, 1904.
4. The Rev. J. A. Milburn in *Commoner,* April 6, 1906; *Nation,* Aug. 4, 1904, and Nov. 2, 1905; "Oriental indifference" in *Living Age,* Oct. 22, 1904; *Florida Times-Union,* Dec. 28, 1904; *New York American* quoted in *Literary Digest,* August 6, 1904.
5. Cassini to Hay, August 2, 1904, box no. 26, Hay Papers, Library of Congress, Washington, D.C.; Howard K. Beale, *Theodore Roosevelt and the Rise of America to World Power* (Baltimore, 1956), pp. 179–80; "personal horror" in *Providence Daily Journal,* July 29, 1904.
6. *New York Times,* Jan. 28, 1905.
7. *Providence Daily Journal,* Nov. 22, 1904; *Nation,* Nov. 24, 1904; *North American Review* (Jan. 1905): 147–54; *Forum* (Jan. 1905): 343; *Review of Reviews* (Jan. 1905): 5–6.
8. *Nation,* Jan. 5, 1905; *Chicago Evening Post,* Dec. 29, 1904.
9. *World's Work* (Nov. 1904): 5334.
10. *Newark Daily Advertiser,* Jan. 5, 1905.
11. R. W. Postgate, *Revolution from 1789 to 1906* (New York, 1962), p. 365.
12. Ibid.
13. Ibid.; Canvas in Vladimir S. Woytinsky, *Stormy Passage* (New York, 1961), p. 14.
14. Postgate, *Revolution,* p. 368.

15. *Hartford Daily Courant,* Jan. 26, 1905; R. R. Rosen, *Forty Years of Diplomacy,* 2 vols. (London, 1922), I: 254.

16. *Outlook,* Jan. 28, 1905; *Commoner,* Feb. 3, 1905.

17. "No virtues" in *St. Paul Pioneer Press,* Jan. 24, 1905; Steffens in *Collier's,* April 22, 1905; Mark Twain, "The Tsar's Sililoquy," *North American Review* (March 1905): 321–6; Philip S. Foner, *Mark Twain: Social Critic* (New York, 1958), p. 119.

18. *Cincinnati Enquirer,* Jan. 23, 1905; *New York Times,* Jan. 30, May 10, 1905.

19. Hay Diary, Jan. 24, 1905, Hay Papers; *World Today* (May 1905): 479–86, and (June 1905): 567.

20. McCormick to Hay, Jan. 31, 1905, *Despatches from U.S. Ministers to Russia, 1808–1906* (National Archives, Washington, D.C.: micro. roll no. 62); advice to correspondent in "Foreign Diplomats Concerning the Revolution of 1905," *Krasnyi Arkhiv* LIII (1932): 151–2.

21. *Saturday Evening Post,* May 27, 1905.

3. Wild to Go to Russia

1. Trepov in *New York Evening Journal,* Jan. 27, 1905; Harry Rogoff, *East Side Epic: The Life and Work of Meyer London* (New York, 1930), p. 25.

2. All material on Miliukov's tour from *New York Times,* Dec. 20, 23, 1904, Jan. 15, 19, Feb. 27, 1905; *New York Sun,* Dec. 13, 1904, Jan. 25, March 7, 8, 1905; *Hull House Bulletin* VII, no. 1 (1905–06): 22–3; some of his speeches in Paul Miliukov, *Russia and Its Crisis* (Chicago, 1905).

3. Morris Hilquit, *Loose Leaves from a Busy Life* (New York, 1934), pp. 107–8.

4. *Jewish Independent,* July 13, 1906; *East Side House Bulletin* II, no. 22.

5. Lillian D. Wald, *The House on Henry Street* (New York, 1915), pp. 229, 238, 248; Beryl Williams, *Lillian Wald: Angel of Henry Street* (New York, 1948), pp. 145–6.

6. Walling to A. Strunsky, June 26, 1905, Walling Papers, State Historical Society of Wisconsin, Madison, Wis.; Ernest Poole, *The Bridge: My Own Story* (New York, 1940), pp. 112, 171.

7. Rogoff, *East Side Epic*, p. 25; Moses Rischin, *The Promised City: New York's Jews, 1810–1914* (Cambridge, Mass., 1962), pp. 163–4; Emma Goldman, *Living My Life* (New York, 1934), p. 359; *Harper's Weekly*, Dec. 31, 1904; *St. Louis Post-Dispatch*, Jan. 24, 1905.

8. *Saturday Evening Post*, Feb. 24, 1906.

9. Goldman, *Living My Life*, pp. 360–1; Alice Stone Blackwell, ed., *The Little Grandmother of the Russian Revolution: Reminiscences and Letters of Catherine Breshkovsky* (Boston, 1917), p. 125.

10. Goldman, *Living My Life*, 360–1.

11. Wald, *House on Henry Street*, pp. 238–40; Poole, *The Bridge*, pp. 103–4; Howe in Blackwell, *Breshkovsky*, p. 123; *St. Louis Post-Dispatch*, Jan. 24, 1905.

12. *Social Democratic Herald*, Feb. 11, 1905; *Chicago Examiner*, Jan. 30, 1905; *Chicago American*, Jan. 25, 1905; accounts of other appearances in Blackwell, *Breshkovsky*, pp. 111–22.

13. Blackwell, *Breshkovsky*, pp. 130–2; Goldman, *Living My Life*, p. 364.

14. *Chicago Tribune*, Jan. 24, 1905; *St. Louis Post-Dispatch*, Jan. 24, 1905.

15. Paxton Hibben, *The Peerless Leader, William Jennings Bryan* (New York, 1929), pp. 243–5, 265–75; *Commoner*, April 16, May 20, July 2, 1905, Oct. 21, 1906.

16. Poole, *The Bridge*, p. 112; *William English Walling: A Symposium* (New York, 1938), pp. 10, 39, 40–1; "draw inspiration" in "American Social Workers in Russia," *Charities and the Commons*, Dec. 1, 1906.

17. Poole, *The Bridge*, pp. 113, 171; *East Side House Bulletin* II, nos. 3, 4.
18. Poole, *The Bridge*, pp. 114–15; idem, "Maxim Gorky in New York," *Slavonic and East European Review* XXII (May 1944); *Walling: A Symposium*, p. 27.
19. Poole, *The Bridge*, pp. 103, 116–19; idem, "Maxim Gorky in New York."
20. Poole, *The Bridge*, pp. 128–69.
21. Ibid., p. 169.
22. *Walling: A Symposium*, pp. 10–11; Walling to his mother, Oct. 23, Nov. 28, Dec. 25, 1905, Jan. 29, 1906, Walling Papers.
23. Richard O'Connor, *Jack London: A Biography* (Boston, 1964), pp. 134–5, 222–4.
24. *Chicago Socialist*, Feb. 11, 25, March 18, 1905.
25. "Social Workers," *Charities and the Commons;* Walling to his father, Feb. 24, April 1, 1906, Walling Papers; account of marriage in *Wilshire's Magazine* (Aug. 1906): 7.
26. *Walling: A Symposium*, p. 10; Walling to his mother, Dec. 25, 1905, Jan. 29, 1906, Walling Papers.
27. Poole, *The Bridge*, p. 168.
28. *Christian Observer*, May 19, 1905.
29. *Hartford Daily Courant*, March 6, 1905; *Kansas City Star*, March 6, 1905; *Nation*, March 9, June 8, 1905; *Tampa Tribune*, March 29, 1905; *Chicago News*, March 16, 1905.
30. *New York Evening Journal*, May 2, 1905.
31. *Presbyterian*, April 5, 1905.
32. Richard Hough, *The Potemkin Mutiny* (London, 1960), p. 17
33. *New York Times*, June 29, 30, Aug. 14, 1905; *Coast Seamen's Journal*, July 12, 1905; *New York Herald*, June 29, 1905.

4. Roosevelt Rescues the Tsar

1. TR to C. A. Spring-Rice, March 19, 1904, Elting E. Morison, ed., *The Letters of Theodore Roosevelt*, 8 vols. (Cambridge, Mass., 1951–54), IV: 760; TR to Spring-Rice, quoted in Howard K. Beale, *Theodore Roosevelt and the Rise of America to World Power* (Baltimore, 1956), p. 264.

2. TR in Beale, *Roosevelt*, pp. 262, 268, and in *Outlook*, June 18, 1904; *Jewish Exponent*, Feb. 24, 1905; *Republican* quoted in *Literary Digest*, Dec. 3, 1904; Jewish prisoners in *American Israelite*, July 27, 1905; *Jewish Independent*, March 9, 1906; Schiff in William A. Williams, *American-Russian Relations, 1781–1947* (New York, 1952), p. 45.

3. Beale, *Roosevelt*, p. 264.

4. Hay Diary, Dec. 6, 1904, Hay Papers, Library of Congress, Washington, D.C.; Frankenstein in McCormick to Albert J. Beveridge, July 21, 1905, Beveridge Papers, Library of Congress, Washington, D.C.

5. TR to George von L. Meyer, Feb. 6, 1905, and to John Hay, April 2, 1905, Morison, *Letters of TR*, IV: 1115, 1158; unsigned memo to TR, Jan. 28, 1905, Letters to TR, Roosevelt Papers, Library of Congress, Washington, D.C.; Meyer's plea in Beale, *Roosevelt*, p. 12.

6. Hay to S. Eddy, June 7, 1904, box no. 20, Hay Papers; Hay Diary, Feb. 6, 1905, Hay Papers; Hay to Cassini, Oct. 5, 1905, and F. B. Loomis to Cassini, Feb. 20, 1904, *Notes to Foreign Legations in the U.S., 1834–1906* (National Archives, Washington, D.C.: micro roll no. 84); Rosen quoted in *Commoner*, June 9, 1905.

7. Beveridge memo, Dec. 14, 1904, Beveridge Papers; Sternberg in Hay Diary, Dec. 6, 1904, Hay Papers; "quiet" in Wharton Barker to Count Lamsdorff, Feb. 9, 1905, Barker Papers, Library of Congress, Washington, D.C.

8. *Congressional Record,* Feb. 20, 1905, 58 Cong., 3 sess., p. 2943. Baker revealed his conversations with the president and the Republican leadership during his House speech.

9. R. R. Rosen, *Forty Years of Diplomacy,* 2 vols. (London, 1922), I: 225–6.

10. Hay, Diary, Dec. 26, 1904, Hay Papers; Meyer Diary, Jan. 7, 21, April 3, 12, 1905, Meyer Papers, Library of Congress, Washington, D.C.

11. TR to Meyer, Dec. 26, 1904, Morison, *Letters of TR,* IV: 1078–9; Meyer to TR, Jan. 28, 1905, Letters to TR, Roosevelt Papers; Meyer to Hay, May 23, 1905, box no. 17, Hay Papers.

12. Meyer to Hay, June 2, 1905, *Despatches from U. S. Ministers to Russia, 1808–1906* (National Archives, Washington, D.C., micro. roll no. 63).

13. Wilhelm II to C. Tower, June 4, 1905, in Letters to TR, Roosevelt Papers.

14. Beale, *Roosevelt,* p. 253; Meyer to Hay, July 3, 7, *Despatches from U. S. Ministers,* micro. roll no. 63; see also Meyer Diary, July 3, 20, 1905, Meyer Papers.

15. TR to Meyer, July 7, 1905, Morison, *Letters of TR,* IV: 1262–3; Mark A. D. Howe, *George von Lengerke Meyer* (New York, 1919), pp. 177–83.

16. Beale, *Roosevelt,* pp. 266–73; TR to Elihu Root, Sept. 14, 1905, Root Papers, Library of Congress, Washington, D.C.

17. *Independent,* Sept. 14, 1905; see also Meyer Diary, Aug. 3, 1905, Meyer Papers.

18. *New York World,* Aug. 3, 1905; *Hartford Daily Courant,* Oct. 26, 1905; Burroughs in *New York Times,* Oct. 29, 1905; DeLeon in *New York Daily People,* Sept. 7, 1905; Philip S. Foner, *Mark Twain: Social Critic* (New York, 1958), pp. 119–20.

19. Root to W. Reid, Sept. 9, 1905, box no. 300, Root Papers;

TR quoted in *Watchman*, Aug. 31, 1905; Beveridge to R. McCormick, Oct. 5, 1905, Beveridge Papers.

20. Meyer to Hay, July 7, 1905, *Despatches from U. S. Ministers*, micro. roll no. 63.

21. *Financial Review*, Aug. 4, 1905; Baroness Rosen in *Presbyterian*, Sept. 20, 1905.

22. *Florida Times-Union*, Aug. 4, 1905. Opinions of Witte in Bernard Pares, *The Fall of the Russian Monarchy* (New York, 1939), p. 86; Stephen Gwynn, ed., *The Letters and Friendships of Sir Cecil Spring-Rice*, 2 vols. (Boston, 1929), 1: 455–9; Kellogg Durland, *The Red Reign* (New York, 1907), p. 18.

23. Sergei Witte, "Count Witte's Memoirs: My Visit to America," *World's Work* (March 1921): 485–86.

24. *Presbyterian*, Aug. 1, 1905; *New York Herald*, July 30, Aug. 16, 18, 1905; *Springfield Republican*, Aug. 5, 1905; Howe, *Meyer*, p. 192; TR to Spring-Rice, Nov. 1, 1905, Morison, *Letters of TR*, v: 61–2.

25. E. J. Dillon, *Russia Today and Yesterday* (New York, 1930), pp. 8, 27–8; idem, "Sergius Witte," *Review of Reviews* (Sept. 1905): 292–5.

26. *New York Times*, July 23, 1905; *Watchman*, Sept. 14, 1905; *Forum* (Oct. 1905): 172–90; *Independent*, Aug. 24, 1905; *New York Tribune*, Aug. 27, 1905; *St. Louis Post-Dispatch*, Jan. 23, 1906.

27. *Newark Daily Advertiser*, Sept. 8, 1905.

28. Witte, "Memoirs," (Dec. 1920): 140–1.

5. Countermarch

1. *American Israelite*, Sept. 7, 1905.

2. Ibid., Jan. 26, 1904.

3. *Jewish Daily Forward*, Jan. 23, 27, 1905; *Wilshire's Magazine* (July 1905): 5.

4. *New York Herald*, May 9, 1905; *New York Sun*, Sept. 14,

1905; *Proceedings of the General Convention of the Independent Order of B'nai B'rith*, New Orleans, 1905 (New York, 1905), pp. 57–8.

5. *Jewish Comment*, July 21, Oct. 13, 1905; *Jewish Exponent*, Jan. 27, March 2, 1905; *American Israelite*, May 4, 1905.

6. *American Israelite*, July 13, Sept. 7, 1905; Cyrus Adler, *Jacob H. Schiff: His Life and Letters*, 2 vols. (New York, 1929), II: 122.

7. Sergei Witte, "Count Witte's Memoirs: My Visit to America," *World's Work* (Dec. 1920): 139–40.

8. *Review of Reviews* (Sept. 1905): 264–5; Adler, *Schiff*, II: 129–32; Witte, "Memoirs," (Dec. 1920): 144, 163–4, (April 1921): 587–8.

9. *American Israelite*, Aug. 31, 1905; *Menorah* (Aug. 1905): 91–2.

10. Witte, "Memoirs," (Dec. 1920): 169.

11. *American Israelite*, Sept. 28, 1905; *Jewish Exponent*, Sept. 29, 1905; Russian papers quoted in *American Israelite*, Sept. 7, Oct. 19, 1905.

12. *Catholic Standard and Times*, May 6, Sept. 9, Nov. 11, 1905.

13. *Presbyterian*, Feb. 1, March 6, July 26, Nov. 20, 1905; *Watchman*, Feb. 18, Nov. 13, 1905; *Christian Evangelist*, March 30, May 11, 1905; *Lutheran Witness*, May 18, Sept. 21, 1905; *Christian Index*, July 12, 1906.

14. *Watchman*, Aug. 26, 1905; *Christian Advocate*, Dec. 28, 1905; *Presbyterian*, Dec. 6, 1905; *Christian Observer*, March 21, 1906; *Catholic Standard and Times*, Feb. 4, Sept. 2, Nov. 4, 1905.

15. *Commercial and Financial Chronicle*, Nov. 26, 1904; *Living Age*, Aug. 12, 1905; *Chicago Tribune*, Jan. 25, 1905.

16. *New York Times*, Jan. 29, 1905; Vanderlip in *St. Louis Post-Dispatch*, Jan. 24, 1905; *Bradstreet's*, Feb. 4, 1905;

Commercial and Financial Chronicle, Feb. 4, 1905; *American Banker*, March 18, 1905.

17. *Jewish Comment*, Oct. 13, 1905; *New York Evening Journal*, May 17, 1905.

18. Witte in *American Industries*, Sept. 15, 1905; *American Exporter*, Oct. 1, 1905; Dun's Review (Oct. 1905): 17–18.

19. William A. Williams, *American-Russian Relations, 1781–1947* (New York, 1952), pp. 82–3; *Bradstreet's*, Sept. 23, Oct. 7, 26, 1905; *American Exporter*, Oct. 1, 8, 1905.

20. *United Mine Workers' Journal*, Feb. 2, 1905.

21. *Elevator Constructor* (April 1905): 20; *New York Evening Journal*, May 17, 1905.

22. *Elevator Constructor* (June 1905): 20–1.

23. *Coast Seamen's Journal*, March 29, 1905; *Lather* (June 1906): 25; *Knights of Labor Journal* (Jan. 1906, Dec. 1906); *United Mine Workers' Journal*, Nov. 18, 1905.

24. Samuel Gompers, *Seventy Years of Life and Labor*, 2 vols. (New York, 1925), II: 46–7; Gompers to Walling, April 7, 1905, and to Friends of Russian Freedom, April 18, 1905, letterbook no. 99, Gompers Papers, New York Public Library, New York, N.Y.

25. *Proceedings of the Twenty-Fifth Annual Convention of the American Federation of Labor*, Pittsburgh, 1905 (Washington, D.C., 1905), pp. 88, 175; *United Mine Workers' Journal*, Feb. 8, 1906.

26. *California Cultivator*, Feb. 4, 1905; *Kansas Farmer*, Jan. 26, Feb. 23, Aug. 30, 1905, Dec. 13, 1906; *Homestead*, March 2, 1905; *Farm, Stock, and Home*, Feb. 15, 1906.

27. *Chicago News*, Oct. 12, 1905.

28. *Proceedings of the Annual Convention of the National Association of Manufacturers*, Atlanta, 1905 (New York, n.d.), pp. 37–9. *Square Deal* (Aug. 1905): 15; *Toledo Socialist*, Nov. 6, 1905.

29. DeLeon in *New York Weekly People*, Feb. 14, 25, 1905.

30. David Shannon, *The Socialist Party of America* (New York, 1955), p. 61; William Z. Foster, *From Bryan to Stalin* (New York, 1937), p. 29; C. H. Kerr to Hilquit, Oct. 4, 1905, Hilquit Papers, State Historical Society of Wisconsin, Madison, Wis.; *Wilshire's Magazine* (March 1905): 5; Debs in *Social Democratic Herald,* March 4, 1905.

31. *New York Weekly People,* April 29, 1905; *Bill Haywood's Book: The Autobiography of William D. Haywood* (New York, 1929), pp. 186–7; Haywood's contribution in *Miner's Magazine,* Nov. 30, 1905; *Worker,* Aug. 5, Nov. 4, Dec. 30, 1905.

32. *New York Weekly People,* Dec. 23, 1905.

33. Ibid., Jan. 27, 1906; *Worker,* Jan. 13, 27, 1906; *Chicago Socialist,* Jan. 13, 27, 1906.

6. We Should Not Have Come Here

1. Bernard Pares, *The Fall of the Russian Monarchy* (New York, 1939), p. 89.

2. Vladimir S. Woytinsky, *Stormy Passage* (New York, 1961), pp. 30–42; Pares, *Russian Monarchy,* p. 89.

3. Pares, *Russian Monarchy,* p. 89.

4. *Worker,* Nov. 4, 1905; *Jewish Daily Forward,* Oct. 31, 1905; *Toledo Socialist* quoted in *Miner's Magazine,* Nov. 30, 1905; Emma Goldman, *Living My Life* (New York, 1934), p. 372.

5. TR to W. Reid, Oct. 31, 1905, letterbook no. 29, Roosevelt Papers, Library of Congress, Washington, D.C.; *New York Herald,* Nov. 13, 1905; *Independent,* Nov. 30, 1905; *Nation,* Dec. 21, 1905.

6. Eddy's September and October despatches, *Despatches from U.S. Ministers to Russia, 1808–1906* (National Archives, Washington, D.C.: micro. roll no. 64); Root to Eddy, Oct. 29, 1905, *Foreign Relations of the United*

States, vol. 1905, p. 776; Paul V. Harper, ed., *The Russia I Believe In: The Memoirs of Samuel N. Harper* (Chicago, 1945), pp. 61–70.

7. Golf in Harper, *Russia*, pp. 60–1; oil in *Bradstreet's*, Sept. 23, 1905; electricity and locomotives in *New York Times*, Oct. 25, 1905; railway in *Knights of Labor Journal* (April 1906); *Washington Post* quoted in *Literary Digest*, Nov. 18, 1905; farm equipment in *American Exporter*, March 1, 1906; sewing machines in Meyer Diary, June 16, 1906, Meyer Papers, Library of Congress, Washington, D.C.

8. *American Exporter*, Oct. 28, 1905; May 1, 1906.

9. *New York Times*, May 20, 1905; Meyer to Hay, May 10, 1905, and F. B. Loomis to Secretary of the Navy, May 29, 1905, both in Office of the Secretary of the Navy, (1904–06), record group 45, no. 19849, National Archives, Washington, D.C.; George S. Queen, "The United States and the Material Advance of Russia" (Ph.D. diss., University of Illinois, 1941), p. 192.

10. *New York Times*, Oct. 21, 23, 25, Nov. 5, 1905; *American Banker*, Oct. 6, 1906; *Bradstreet's*, Oct. 20, Nov. 4, 1905; see also William A. Williams, *American-Russian Relations, 1781–1947* (New York, 1952), p. 54.

11. *Chicago Examiner*, Oct. 29, 1905; *Commercial and Financial Chronicle*, Nov. 1, 1905; Kellogg Durland, *The Red Reign* (New York, 1907), p. 493.

12. Woytinsky, *Stormy Passage*, p. 24.

13. *Bradstreet's*, Nov. 4, 1905; *Financial Review* (Feb. 1906): 24; Williams, *American-Russian Relations*, pp. 53–5.

14. Williams, *American-Russian Relations*, p. 54.

15. *New York Times*, Oct. 25, 27, 31, 1905.

16. Eddy to Root, Oct. 27, 1905, *Despatches from U. S. Ministers*, micro. roll no. 64.

17. All information on the Petrov episode from Woytinsky, *Stormy Passage*, pp. 24–6.

18. Eddy to Root, Nov. 6, 1905, *Despatches from U. S. Ministers*, micro, roll no. 64; *New York Times*, Oct. 31, Nov. 2, 3, 4, 8, 1905.
19, Pares, *Russian Monarchy*, pp. 85–90.
20. Ibid., p. 86.
21. Spring-Rice to Mrs. TR, Nov. 1, 1905, Letters to TR, Roosevelt Papers; Witte in *Chicago Inter-Ocean*, Oct. 31, 1905.
22. *Farmer's Guide*, Nov. 11, 1905; *Tampa Tribune*, Nov. 1, 1905; *Chicago Tribune*, Nov. 6, 1905; *Watchman*, Nov. 9, 1905; *Christian Advocate*, Nov. 9, 1905; *Saturday Evening Post*, Jan. 27, 1906; *New York Times*, Nov. 1 1905; *Painter and Decorator* (Nov. 1905): 660.
23. *Detroit News*, Nov. 2, 1904; *World Today* (Dec. 1905): 1255–6; *Christian Advocate*, Nov. 23, 1905; *Chicago Tribune*, Nov. 3, 1905; *Coast Seamen's Journal*, Nov. 15, 1905.
24. *Jewish Comment*, Nov. 3, 1905.

7. The Pogrom

1. Salo W. Baron, *The Russian Jew Under Tsars and Soviets* (New York, 1964), pp. 67–70; R. W. Postgate, *Revolution from 1789 to 1906* (New York, 1962), pp. 372–80.
2. Vladimir S. Woytinsky, *Stormy Passage* (New York, 1961), pp. 52–3; Baron, *Russian Jew*, p. 69.
3. *Menorah* (Nov. 1905): 244.
4. Ibid., pp. 245–6, 275–7; *Jewish Comment*, Dec. 8, 1905; *American Israelite*, Nov. 16, 1905.
5. *New York Times*, Nov. 18, 24, 1905; *Jewish Comment*, Dec. 8, 1905.
6. *New York Times*, Nov. 9, 13, 17, Dec. 3, 19, 1905; Morris D. Waldman to A. W. Thompson, Feb. 8, 1963.
7. *New York Times*, Nov. 16, 20, 26, 27, 29, 30, 1905; *Jewish Comment*, Nov. 17, 1905; *Presbyterian*, Dec. 13, 1905; *American Hebrew*, Dec. 8, 1905.

8. *Menorah* (Nov. 1905): 250–2; *New York Times*, Nov. 10, 22, 1905.
9. *Jewish Daily Forward*, Nov. 11, 1905.
10. *American Israelite*, Nov. 16, Dec. 6, 1905; *New York Times*, Nov. 16, 1905.
11. *New York Evening Journal*, Nov. 4, 5, 7, 14, 1905; see also Moses Rischin, *The Promised City: New York's Jews, 1810–1914* (Cambridge, Mass., 1962), pp. 229–30; *New York Herald*, Nov. 8, 17, 1905.
12. Stanley Washburn, *The Cable Game* (Boston, 1912), pp. 104–5; *Chicago Inter-Ocean*, Dec. 26, 1905; *Christian Register* quoted in *American Hebrew*, Dec. 8, 1905; *New York Sun*, Nov. 6, 1905; *Vogue* quoted in *Literary Digest*, Nov. 25, 1905 (see correction on p. 867 of quote on p. 774).
13. *Houston Post*, Nov. 15, 1905; *Chicago News*, Nov. 18, 1905.
14. *Jewish Exponent*, Nov. 18, 25, 1905.
15. *Review of Reviews* editorial copybooks, 1904–06, New York Public Library, New York, N.Y., no. 27 (1905).
16. Meyer Diary, Nov. 10, 1905, Meyer Papers, Library of Congress, Washington, D.C.
17. Ibid., Nov. 6, 13, 1905; TR to Meyer, Nov. 9, 1905, letterbook no. 29, Roosevelt Papers, Library of Congress, Washington, D.C.
18. Meyer Diary, Nov. 28, 30, Dec. 6, 1905, Meyer Papers; Meyer to Root, Nov. 30, Dec. 5, 1905, *Despatches from U.S. Ministers to Russia, 1808–1906* (National Archives, Washington, D.C.: micro. rolls no. 64, 65).
19. Eddy to Root, Nov. 5, 16, 18, 25, *Despatches from U.S. Ministers*, micro. roll no. 64; "Consular Letters: Riga, Rostov, Odessa" (Nov., Dec. 1905), record group 59, National Archives, Washington, D.C.; *New York Sun*, Nov. 22, 24, 1905.
20. "Consular letters: Warsaw" (Nov. 1905, Feb. 1906).
21. Ibid., "Odessa" (Nov., Dec. 1905); Eddy to Root, Nov. 6,

1905, *Despatches from U.S. Ministers*, micro. roll no. 64.

22. Meyer Diary, Dec. 9, 1905, Meyer Papers; Meyer to Root, Dec. 6, 12, 1905, *Despatches from U.S. Ministers*, micro. roll no. 65.

23. *New York Times*, Nov. 12, 1905; *Menorah* (Nov. 1905): 253; *Jewish Daily Forward*, Nov. 7, 1905; Miss Dorée in *Miner's Magazine*, Oct. 19, 1905.

24. *Jewish Comment*, Nov. 17, 1905; *New York Times*, Nov. 11, 17, 1905; Cyrus Adler, *Jacob H. Schiff: His Life and Letters*, 2 vols. (New York, 1929), II: 136–8.

25. *Jewish Comment*, Nov. 10, 1905.

26. Tyler Dennett, *John Hay* (New York, 1934), p. 401; Philip C. Jessup, *Elihu Root*, 2 vols. (New York, 1938), II: 65; TR to O. Straus, April 13, 1906, letterbook no. 33, Roosevelt Papers; *Nation*, June 28, 1906.

27. *New York Times*, Nov. 7, 8, 1905; *Menorah* (Nov. 1905): 249–50, 262; *Jewish Comment*, Nov. 10, 17, 1905.

28. Ibid.

29. *New York Times*, Nov. 8, 1905; TR to Straus, Dec. 14, 1905, letterbook no. 30, Roosevelt Papers.

30. TR to Straus, Dec. 14, 1905, letterbook no. 30, Roosevelt Papers; TR to Schiff, Dec. 14, 1905, Letterbook no. 30, Roosevelt Papers; *Menorah* (Nov. 1905): 246–7; TR to Straus, April 10, 1906, Straus Papers, Library of Congress, Washington, D.C.

31. House Committee on Foreign Affairs, "Papers Accompanying Bills and Resolutions," record group 233 (HR-59A-D6), Dec. 11, 1905, National Archives, Washington, D.C.

32. Ibid.

33. *Congressional Record*, June 22, 1906, 59 Cong., 1 sess., p. 8919.

8. A Triumph for Righteousness

1. Meyer Diary, Dec. 28, 1905, Meyer Papers, Library of Congress, Washington, D.C.; R. W. Postgate, *Revolution from 1789 to 1906* (New York, 1962), pp. 357–8, 384–90; Bernard Pares, *The Fall of the Russian Monarchy* (New York, 1939), pp. 88–91.

2. Meyer Diary, Dec. 15, 24, 1905, Meyer Papers; Mark A. O. Howe, *George von Lengerke Meyer* (New York, 1919), pp. 231–2, 275, 285–8; Meyer to Root, Dec. 11, 1905, *Despatches from U.S. Ministers to Russia, 1808–1906* (National Archives, Washington, D.C.: micro. roll no. 65).

3. T. C. Purdy to Meyer, Dec. 15, 1905, and Meyer Diary, Jan. 27, 1906, Meyer Papers; George S. Queen, "The United States and the Material Advance of Russia" (Ph.D. diss., University of Illinois, 1941), pp. 84–5.

4. Meyer Diary, Dec. 30, 1905, Meyer Papers; Bornholdt to Meyer, Jan. 3, 1906, *Despatches from U.S. Ministers*, micro. roll no. 65.

5. Postgate, *Revolution*, pp. 383–90; *Detroit News*, Dec. 27, 1905.

6. Postgate, *Revolution*, pp. 383–90; Pares, *Russian Monarchy*, p. 91; *New York Times*, Dec. 26–31, 1905.

7. *New York Times*, Dec. 3, 1905; *Chicago Tribune*, Dec. 28, 1905; *St. Paul Pioneer Press*, Dec. 25, 1905; *Seattle Daily Times*, Dec. 30, 1905; *Outlook*, Jan. 6, 1906; *Atlanta Journal*, Dec. 28, 1905; Stanley Washburn, *The Cable Game*, (Boston, 1912), pp. 100–1.

8. *Jewish Exponent*, Jan. 3, 1906; *Chicago Socialist*, Jan. 6, 20, 1906.

9. Ernest Poole, *The Bridge: My Own Story* (New York, 1940), pp. 172–3; idem, "Maxim Gorky in New York," *Slavonic and East European Review* XXII (May 1944): 78; Walling to his mother, Dec. 25, 1905, Jan. 29, 1906,

Walling Papers, State Historical Society of Wisconsin, Madison, Wis.

10. *Outlook*, Dec. 15, 1905; *Menorah* (Dec. 1906): 297–8; *American Israelite*, June 28, 1906; *Farmer's Review*, Dec. 15, 1906; *Jewish Independent*, Aug. 31, 1906.

11. *Washington Post* in *Literary Digest*, Sept. 8, 1906; *Menorah* (Nov. 1906): 233–5; *Independent*, April 25, May 16, 1907.

12. *Collier's*, May 19, 1906; *Chicago News*, June 23, 1906; Poole, *The Bridge*, pp. 174–6.

13. Albert B. Paine, *Mark Twain: A Biography*, 3 vols. (New York, 1912), II: 291–4; *Independent*, Dec. 19, 1907.

14. *New York Herald*, Feb. 12, 1905; *Collier's* April 8, 1905; *Everybody's*, (April 1905): 502.

15. Except where otherwise noted, details of the Gorky tour are from Philip S. Foner, *Mark Twain: Social Critic* (New York, 1958); Filia Holtzman, "A Mission that Failed: Gorky in America," *Slavic and East European Journal* VII (Fall 1962): 227–36; William Dean Howells, *My Mark Twain* (New York, 1910); Alexander Kaun, *Maxim Gorky and His Russia* (New York, 1931); Paine, *Mark Twain;* Poole, *The Bridge;* idem, "Maxim Gorky in New York."

16. *New York Sun*, April 11, 1906.

17. *Brooklyn Eagle*, April 15, 1906.

18. Ibid.

19. Ibid., April 16, 1906; *New York Times*, April 16, 1906.

20. *Brooklyn Eagle*, April 15, 1906.

21. *Pittsburgh Sun*, April 16, 1906.

22. *New York Press*, April 20, 1906.

23. *Presbyterian*, April 25, Aug. 8, 1906; *New York Sun*, April 18, 1906.

24. *New York Commercial Advertiser*, April 18, 1906.

25. "Chicago women" in *New York Tribune*, April 15, 1906; *Chicago Inter-Ocean*, May 2, 1906.

26. *New York Times*, April 15, 21, 1906; *New York Com-*

mercial Advertiser, April 23, 1906; *New York World,* April 20, 1906.

27. *Wilshire's Magazine* (May 1906): 1, 10, 17.
28. James W. Linn, *Jane Addams: A Biography* (New York, 1935), p. 223.
29. *Chicago Inter-Ocean,* May 6, 1906; *New York Press,* April 29, May 3, 1906.
30. *Jewish Exponent,* July 30, 1906; *Jewish Independent,* Aug. 16, 1906.
31. Meyer Diary, May 11, 1906, Meyer Papers; Root to Meyer, June 23, 1906, *Diplomatic Instructions of the Department of State, 1801–1906* (National Archives, Washington, D.C.: micro. roll no. 140, 1906).
32. Denunciations reported in *Independent,* April 26, 1906; *London Daily Telegraph,* July 2, 5, 1906; "Foreign Diplomats Concerning the Revolution of 1905," *Krasnyi Arkhiv* LIII (1932): 151.
33. Authors in *Independent,* April 26, 1906; view that some had seen U.S. as hypocritical recalled by Mrs. Vladimir Woytinsky in an interview, Aug. 3, 1962, Washington, D.C.; Simkhovich in *Political Science Quarterly* (Dec. 1906): 569–95; Tolstoy in *Living Age,* March 17, 1906; *Vilna Hasunan* quoted in *American Israelite,* July 16, 1906.
34. *Christian Advocate,* Sept. 21, 1906; *American Israelite,* June 28, Aug, 6, 1906; *Outlook,* March 9, 1907; *Menorah* (July 1906): 12; *Painter and Decorator,* Aug. 2, 1906.
35. The Miliukov "interview" appeared in no one paper; its present arrangement is based upon terse comments quoted in *Jewish Comment,* Jan. 19, 26, 1908; *Jewish Daily Forward,* Jan. 22, 23, 25, 27, 1908; *New York Press,* Jan. 16, 17, 1908; *New York Sun,* Jan. 16, 1908; *New York Commercial Advertiser,* Jan. 17, 1908; see also "The Miliukov Incident," *Independent,* Jan. 23, 1908.
36. *Independent,* Jan. 23, 1908; *Review of Reviews* (Feb. 1908): 149–51; *New York Press,* Jan. 19, 1908.

Bibliography

Unpublished Sources

STATE DEPARTMENT BRANCH, NATIONAL ARCHIVES: *Despatches from U.S. Ministers to Russia, 1808–1906,* microfilm publication no. 35, rolls no. 61–66 (March 5, 1904–Aug. 14 1906); *Diplomatic Instructions of the Department of State, 1801–1906,* microfilm publication no. 77, roll no. 140 (Russia, Feb. 14, 1898–Aug. 14, 1906); *Notes to Foreign Legations in the U.S., 1834–1906,* microfilm publication no. 99, roll no. 84 (Russia, Feb. 8, 1898–Aug. 10, 1906); "Notes Received from Foreign Legations: Russia," record group 59; "Consular letters: St. Petersburg, Moscow, Warsaw, Odessa, Riga, Rostov" (Jan. 1, 1940–Aug. 14, 1906), record group 59.

NAVY DEPARTMENT BRANCH, NATIONAL ARCHIVES: Office of the Secretary (1904–1906), record group 45.

LEGISLATIVE BRANCH, NATIONAL ARCHIVES: House Committee on Foreign Affairs, 58th and 59th Congresses; "Petitions and Memorials" and "Papers Accompanying Bills and Resolutions" (H6-H7 and D6-D7), record group 233.

COLLECTIONS OF PAPERS: Wharton Barker, Albert J. Beveridge, John Hay, George von Lengerke Meyer, Theodore Roosevelt, Elihu Root, and Oscar Straus (Library of Congress, Washington, D.C.); Samuel Gompers and Lillian D. Wald (New York Public Library, New York, N.Y.); Morris Hilquit and William E. Walling (State Historical Society of Wisconsin, Madison, Wis.).

INTERVIEWS: With Norman Thomas (New York, N.Y., Aug. 6, 1962); with Mrs. Vladimir Woytinsky (Washington, D.C., Aug. 3, 1962).

CORRESPONDENCE: From Upton Sinclair (Sept. 4, 14, 1962); from Morris D. Waldman (Feb. 8, 9, 1963).

MISCELLANEOUS: *Review of Reviews* editorial copybooks, 1904–1906, New York Public Library, New York, N.Y.; George S. Queen, "The United States and the Material Advance of Russia," (Ph.D. diss., University of Illinois, 1941).

Published Records

Foreign Relations of the United States, vols. 1904–1906; *Congressional Record*, 58th and 59th Congresses.

Contemporary Sources

ORGANIZATIONS: *National Convention of the Socialist Party, Chicago, 1904* (Chicago, 1904); *Proceedings of the Twenty-Fifth Annual Convention of the American Federation of Labor, Pittsburgh, 1905* (Washington, D.C., 1905); *Proceedings of the General Convention of the Independent Order of B'nai B'rith, New Orleans, 1905* (New York, 1905); *Proceedings of the Annual Convention of the National Association of Manufacturers, Atlanta, 1905* (New York, n.d.).

PERIODICALS: *Arena, Bookman, Collier's, Commoner, Everybody's, Forum, Harper's Monthly, Harper's Weekly, Inde-*

pendent, *International Quarterly, Literary Digest, Living Age, McClure's, Nation, North American Review, Outlook, Political Science Quarterly, Review of Reviews, Saturday Evening Post, Square Deal, Vogue, World's Work, World Today.*

NEWSPAPERS: *Atlanta Journal;* Boston *Recorder, Register,* and *Transcript; Brooklyn Eagle;* Chicago *American, Evening Post, Examiner, Inter-Ocean, News,* and *Tribune; Cincinnati Enquirer; Detroit News; Florida Times-Union; Hartford Daily Courant; Houston Post; Kansas City Star; London Daily Telegraph; National Intelligencer; Newark Daily Advertiser;* New York *American, Commercial Advertiser, Evening Journal, Herald, Post, Press, Sun, Times, Tribune,* and *World; Pittsburgh Sun; Providence Daily Journal; St. Louis Post-Dispatch; St. Louis Pioneer Press; Seattle Daily Times; Springfield* (Mass.) *Republican; Tampa* (Fla.) *Tribune; Washington Post.*

SPECIAL: *American Hebrew, American Israelite, Jewish Comment, Jewish Exponent, Jewish Independent, Menorah.*

Catholic Mirror, Catholic News, Catholic Standard and Times, Catholic World.

Christian Index and *Watchman* (Baptist), *Christian Evangelist* (Christian), *Lutheran Witness, Christian Advocate* (Methodist), *Presbyterian* and *Christian Observer* (Presbyterian).

Charities and the Commons, East Side House Bulletin, Hull House Bulletin.

American Federationist, Blacksmith's Journal, Coast Seamen's Journal, Elevator Constructor, Knights of Labor Journal, Lather, Meatcutter's Journal, Painter and Decorator, Seattle Union Record, Shoe Worker's Journal, United Mine Workers' Journal.

American Agriculturist, California Cultivator, Farmer's Guide, Farmer's Review, Farm, Stock, and Home, Homestead, Kansas Farmer.

Appeal to Reason, Chicago Socialist, International So-cialist Review, Jewish Daily Forward, Miner's Magazine, New York Daily People, New York Weekly People, Social Democratic Herald, Toledo Socialist, Wilshire's Magazine, The Worker.

American Banker, American Exporter, American In-dustries, Bradstreet's, Commercial and Financial Chronicle, Dun's Review, Financial Review.

Memoirs

E. J. Dillon, *Russia Today and Yesterday* (New York, 1930); Kellogg Durland, *The Red Reign* (New York, 1907); William Z. Foster, *From Bryan to Stalin* (New York, 1937); Emma Goldman, *Living My Life* (New York, 1934); Samuel Gom-pers, *Seventy Years of Life and Labor*, 2 vols. (New York, 1925); *Bill Haywood's Book: The Autobiography of William D. Haywood* (New York, 1929); Morris Hilquit, *Loose Leaves from a Busy Life* (New York, 1934); Adolf Kraus, *Reminis-cences and Comments* (Chicago, 1925); Ernest Poole, *The Bridge: My Own Story* (New York, 1940); Baron R. R. Rosen, *Forty Years of Diplomacy*, 2 vols. (London, 1922); Upton Sinclair, *Autobiography* (New York, 1962); Lillian D. Wald, *The House on Henry Street* (New York, 1915); Stanley Washburn, *The Cable Game* (Boston, 1912); Sergei Witte, "Count Witte's Memoirs," A. Yarmolinsky, ed., serially in *World's Work* (Nov., Dec., 1920; Jan., Feb., March, April, 1921); Vladimir S. Woytinsky, *Stormy Passage* (New York, 1961).

Edited Letters and Biographies

Cyrus Adler, *Jacob H. Schiff: His Life and Letters*, 2 vols. (New York, 1929); Howard K. Beale, *Theodore Roosevelt and the Rise of America to World Power* (Baltimore, 1956);

Alice Stone Blackwell, ed., *The Little Grandmother of the Russian Revolution: Reminiscences and Letters of Catherine Breshkovsky* (Boston, 1917); Tyler Dennett, *John Hay* (New York, 1934); Philip S. Foner, *Mark Twain: Social Critic* (New York, 1958); Ray Ginger, *The Bending Cross: A Biography of Eugene V. Debs* (New Brunswick, N.J., 1949); Stephen Gwynn, ed., *The Letters and Friendships of Sir Cecil Spring-Rice*, 2 vols. (Boston, 1929); Paul V. Harper, ed., *The Russia I Believe In: The Memoirs of Samuel N. Harper* (Chicago, 1945); Paxton Hibben, *The Peerless Leader, William Jennings Bryan* (New York, 1929); Mark A. D. Howe, *George von Lengerke Meyer* (New York, 1919); William Dean Howells, *My Mark Twain* (New York, 1910); Philip C. Jessup, *Elihu Root*, 2 vols. (New York, 1938); Alexander Kaun, *Maxim Gorky and His Russia* (New York, 1931); James W. Linn, *Jane Addams: A Biography* (New York, 1935); Elting E. Morison, ed., *The Letters of Theodore Roosevelt*, 8 vols. (Cambridge, Mass., 1951–1954); Richard O'Connor, *Jack London: A Biography* (Boston, 1964); Albert B. Paine, *Mark Twain: A Biography*, 3 vols. (New York, 1912); Arnold Petersen, *Daniel DeLeon: Social Architect* (New York, 1941); Harry Rogoff, *East Side Epic: The Life and Work of Meyer London* (New York, 1930); *William English Walling: A Symposium* (New York, 1938); Beryl Williams, *Lillian Wald: Angel of Henry Street* (New York, 1948).

Articles

William L. Burton, "Revolution and American Mythology," *Midwest Quarterly* IV (Winter 1963): 79–89; George L. Cherry, "American Metropolitan Press Reaction to the Paris Commune of 1871," *Mid-America* XXXII (Jan. 1950): 3–12; Merle Curti, "The Impact of the Revolutions of 1848 on American Thought," *Proceedings of the American Philosophical Society* XCIII (June 1949): 209–15; "Foreign Diplomats

Concerning the Revolution of 1905," *Krasnyi Arkhiv* LIII
(1932): 151–58; Filia Holtzman, "A Mission that Failed:
Gorky in America," *Slavic and East European Journal* VII
(Fall 1962): 227–36; Ernest Poole, "Maxim Gorky in New
York," *Slavonic and East European Review* XXII (May 1944):
78–88; Stanley K. Schultz, "The Morality of Politics: The
Muckrackers' Vision of Democracy," *Journal of American
History* (Dec. 1965): 527–47; Winston B. Thorson, "Ameri-
can Public Opinion and the Portsmouth Peace Conference,"
American Historical Review LIII (April 1948): 439–64.

Miscellaneous Works

Thomas A. Bailey, *America Faces Russia* (Ithaca, N.Y.,
1950); Thomas A. Bailey, *A Diplomatic History of the Ameri-
can People* (New York, 1955); Salo W. Baron, *The Russian
Jew Under Tsars and Soviets* (New York, 1964); Elgin R.
Coate, *American Trades Unions* (London, 1904); Norman A.
Graebner, *Ideas and Diplomacy* (New York, 1964); Sidney
Harcave, *Russia: A History* (New York, 1952); Richard
Hough, *The Potemkin Mutiny* (London, 1960); Paul Miliu-
kov, *Russia and Its Crisis* (Chicago, 1905); Henry W. Nevin-
son, *The Dawn in Russia* (New York, 1906); Sir Bernard
Pares, *The Fall of the Russian Monarchy* (New York, 1939);
R. W. Postgate, *Revolution from 1789 to 1906* (New York,
1962); Moses Rischin, *The Promised City: New York's Jews,
1810–1914* (Cambridge, Mass., 1962); David Shannon, *The
Socialist Party of America* (New York, 1955); William A.
Williams, *American-Russian Relations, 1781–1947* (New
York, 1952).

Index

Index